Compiled and edited by Peter Goddard and Philip Kamin

With
Bernie Finkelstein, Richard Flohil, John Griffen, Alan Guettel,
Tom Harrison, Dan Hill, Mark Kearney, John Martin, Terry David Mulligan,
Wilder Penfield III, Carole Pope, Greg Quill, Randy Ray,
Juan Rodriguez, Lorraine Segato, David Clayton Thomas.

McGRAW-HILL RYERSON LIMITED
Toronto Montreal

Canadian Cataloguing in Publication Data
Main entry under title:
Shakin' all over
ISBN 0-07-549773-5
1. Popular music - Canada. I. Goddard, Peter.
ML3484.5.S48 1988 784.5'00971 C88-095316-0

Art Direction: Steven Baine/Design UYA Inc.
Production Co-ordination: W M Enterprises

PRODUCED BY GODDARD & KAMIN INC.
for McGraw-Hill Ryerson Limited

CONTENTS

INTRODUCTION

Northern Lights: a snapshot of Canadian pop history

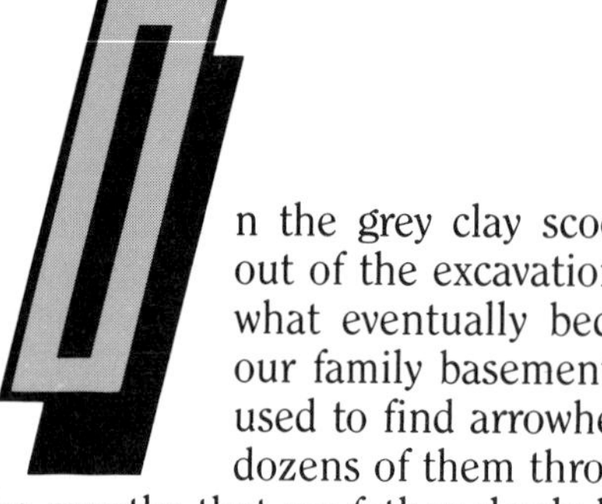

n the grey clay scooped out of the excavation for what eventually became our family basement, we used to find arrowheads, dozens of them throughout the months that my father slowly hammered, nailed, and sawed our house together. We weren't particularly surprised by our discovery, this being old Mississauga Indian turf long before it was claimed by the first generation of suburbanites who'd read *Five Acres and Independence* and headed out to subdivide pastures west of Toronto. We weren't even surprised we weren't surprised.

Certain things came along with growing up in Canada and one was the certainty that change, if any, would be gradual, modest, and in no way upsetting. It was the Americans who were forever in turmoil, not us. In the squat split-level paradise with a breezeway that was Canada in the '50s, things weren't boring exactly; they can never be when you are about 12 or 13 and all your hormones are kicking in at once. Nevertheless, we had no reason to believe things were going to be much different for us than they'd been for our folks. Only later did we see the irony in this, of course, as we came to believe Canada had no history after we'd spent all those restless years trapped in its sludgey flow. For at the time we knew *Hockey Night in Canada* would continue just as surely as the checkout girl at Carload Meats you know, the one who wouldn't let you put your hand under her sweater.

Even in public school we were taught to feel the tug of the land, the gravity from its many histories: *Paddle-To-The-Sea* and all that. So an arrowhead seemed no more remarkable to us than those ancient bones we found. But then, even as kids, we rather knew our place in Canada, our past rolling over us, rolling us over into the future forever. Hey, we knew what was coming up. No sweat. So we lost the arrowheads as casually as we found them; used them as skipping stones across the Credit River that had been their original owners, main route to Lake

Ontario or just as something to throw at the birds in the trees. I grew up living with the past piled all around me, a Canadian true Maple Leaf blue. So what was new?

Some sort of weird rumble on radio, that's what: "Have you heard the news there's good rockin' tonight..."

Looking back. I can see what a remarkable thing it was finding those arrowheads. But I'm looking at them across a kind of great divide that came with what I heard on that tiny radio of mine: a weird discombobilating music that came at me in pieces. Rock 'n' roll.

I didn't know it at the time that that sound signalled something that went well beyond the music itself, a new attitude that I think shaped a new kind of Canada, a country, wired from sea-to-sea, which had one of its borders stretched across the mid-'60s to no more fanfare than Gene Vincent singing "Be-Bop-A-Lula."

In fact, it's taken all these years and this book, *Shakin' All Over,* to give us this perspective; to show who shaped the music we grew up with, and how it effected their lives; the stars and the forgotten one-hit wonders; the deejays, veejays, and the movers and shakers in the music business itself.

At the start, rock 'n' roll meant something basic. It was sex/sin/salvation and all the other great unholy stuff we loved. It arrived in our lives like some ultra-mysterious purple ray from deep space, zapping us into another time and space. It showed there were surprises to be had in this grand, endless land of ours. It could be something else as well — a way out. I mean, I wanted to be wherever that stuff was coming from. I didn't mean Memphis or Los Angeles or New York, but in whatever frame of mind that could produce it.

I never made it, not really. I did my hair right. I had the attitude down. But years spent in bands only taught me that I'd never play piano as well as Ray Charles. However, years spent as a rock 'n' roll critic took me close to those who were there, and in knowing them I came to understand this other history of Canada, the history of its rock 'n' roll and the effect it had.

They're all in this book. And as different as they are, they all have something in common: none of them, as far as I know, ever felt that Canada was anywhere but on the front lines when it came to rock 'n' roll.

Juan Rodriguez was probably the first writer anywhere to fashion rock criticism into a form of guerrilla warfare. Wary would be the act coming back to Montreal after he had already passed judgment on them. And there are still those who remember being in the same movie theatre the day Neil Young appeared on the screen — and Rodriguez stomping down the aisles letting everyone in on exactly what he thought of the star attraction.

I have never been with Lorraine Segato except to find a never-ending stream of people coming by, each to say something private to her. Her band, the Parachute Club, has made every effort to be as public a unit as possible, yet few musicians I've known seem to have reached people so personally as she has. Her turf was/is Toronto's Queen St. West, and its real history won't be written until she writes her's. If she had a mentor, it was Carole Pope, who as much as anyone ever has defined rock 'n' roll in Canada. She's probably the bravest of us all — conjuring her Rich Romance bitch/goddess genie alone and up out of nowhere. I found it difficult to believe the retreating, shy woman I'd talk to for one reason or another. I once tried to talk her into turning "Highschool Confidential" into a ultra-lurid movie that we'd write together. Could she be the same as the leather-snapping dominatrix I'd just seen at the old Colonial on Toronto Yonge St. Strip?

Tom Harrison, the rock critic for the Vancouver *Province*, is no less empassioned. In fact, he's probably the living definition of what the rock critic should be: a savvy writer who never leaves the very streets where the music starts. As a form of extra insurance, he's even formed his own band, Bruno Gerussi's Medallion, which is suffering through all the hassles he's discovered with other bands.

In Montreal, John Griffen has his passion too. There have been no end of nights when one was to meet him in some dark *boite* that, of course, just so happened to feature the latest reggae deejay, reggae band or both.

I can't remember when Richard Flohil wasn't involved to his teeth with music: promotions acts, writing about them, producing them, hanging out with them. No one has been closer to the heart of the business of music in Canada than he has. Now, as the head of the Mariposa Folk Festival, he can wear all his musical hats at once. I also can't remember when Dan Hill, normally a reasoned, soft-spoken man with considered opinions, wasn't getting drawn into some media fracas or another. At a Christmas Eve party I held, one of my best friends at the time felt Dan needed a lecture about song writing, growing up, and a whole bunch of things in between. Damned if she didn't walk over to him across the room and begin the lecture on the spot. As far as I can remember, he didn't say anything then. Later, the incident and, no doubt, others like it, ended up in a song.

There's a secret you should know about Bernie Finkelstein as well. He'd have you believe that he's your typical rock 'n' roll manager whose mystified by what Bruce Cockburn is really up to, and besides, that's not his business anyway. Don't buy it. No one has listened as hard to Canadian folk or pop or rock as he has. I don't mean to just the notes or words, but to what the sense of the song is. Sometimes his acts don't rock 'n' roll, but they've rarely written a bad lyric. And perhaps few writers have ever been as sensitive to the meaning of rock 'n' roll as Finkelstein's collaborator, Wilder Penfield III, the feeling man's critic.

Too often those we take to be our heroes are the ones sold as heroes – today's hot rock flash. As often or not, those behind the scenes have effected the music even more. Terry David Mulligan, actor (*The Accused*), TV star (MuchMusic veejay), deejay (*Toronto, Vancouver*) is the closest rock 'n' roll in this country has to a mentor. His career has taken him from talk radio in Toronto to hosting CBC-TV's *Good Rockin' Tonight*, and not once has he ever flagged in his support of the music – neither True Believer nor cynic, but always the true fan.

John Martin, too, has changed the sound and look of rock more than we'll ever understand. As musical director of MuchMusic, he helped shape the style and spirit of music television, bringing to it a spirit all its own.

The spirit, that's it. That's how rock changed things. I still go back to the old homestead, and, sometimes when we go out for a walk, we'll poke around in galleys on the off-chance I'll find an arrowhead. I haven't. I wish I hadn't been as careless as I was, throwing them away. But I understand why it was so easy for me to do so. And perhaps that's another result of my adventures in rock 'n' roll: by giving me a future I never thought I'd have, I re-discovered a past I once hoped to forget.

* * *

THE BLASTS

They were the singers and bands you heard at local sock hops. It was their singles and albums you put on someone's record player and listened to in the basement. If you were lucky, you saw them play at community halls or at your high school as you danced under the basketball hoops in the gym.

And they were Canadian. In some cases, they may even have been from your hometown or the next city over. Some went on to national and even international fame; others struggled for years on the road, playing in bars and clubs, cherishing the moments when their songs finally got airplay on local radio stations.

Some of these musicians are still at it today; others have left their dreams of stardom behind, their memories recorded in fading newspaper clippings or etched on vinyl.

What do these musical pioneers remember from those golden years when the Canadian music industry was still young?

by Mark Kearney and Randy Ray

1
THE ROAD TO RUIN

by David Clayton Thomas

David Clayton Thomas (centre): and Blood, Sweat and Tears

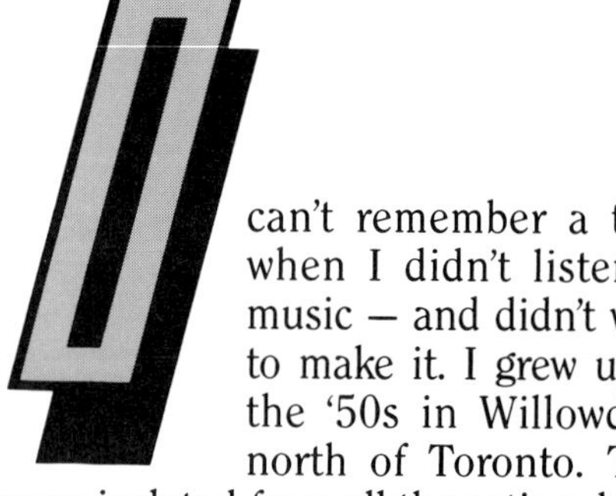

can't remember a time when I didn't listen to music — and didn't want to make it. I grew up in the '50s in Willowdale, north of Toronto. That may seem isolated from all the action, but it wasn't, not really. I had a buddy named Bill (we'd known each other since we were five) and we'd get together late at night and huddle around the radio listening to Bo Diddley and blues and rock coming from radio stations in Buffalo. You couldn't always hear the great music on Toronto stations, at least not then. The deejay we liked best was "The Hound" — George Lorenz was his real name. Other kids would have teenage parties and sit around listening to "How Much Is That Doggie In The Window?" and dance to Pat Boone; at our parties, we'd listen to the Hound.

I was also starting to collect records then, when I was only 12 or 13 years old: Muddy Waters, Lightnin' Hopkins. This was before I started singing, before I had my own bands. I was just a kid. But I knew I loved this music. It just took a bit of time to realize it would be my life. We were 14-year-olds with black leather jackets and motorcycle boots and chains and no motorcycles. We used to park our bicycles down the street and walk to restaurants so people would think we had motorcycles. We were Fonzies, we were greasers. We listened to black music out of Detroit and shit like that. Our role models were James Dean and Marlon Brando and *Rebel Without a Cause*. We were hassled in school because we were outrageous. Crazy kids. We had trouble with our home lives, both of us — Bill not so much as me. At 15, I was already running away. I had no interest in school. We just hung around and smoked cigarettes and talked to the girls. I just didn't know what to do with school, I guess. I was one of those people who constantly got on report cards "extremely bright, but what's the matter with this kid?"

I wasn't doing anything real bad — I was just on the street. I didn't really get into

BLAST

THE BELLS

BACKGROUND:
The Bells were a Montreal-based group that included Cliff Edwards, his then wife Anne (who left The Bells before their big successes), her sister Jacki Ralph, Frank Mills (who departed early for his own successful solo career), Doug Gravelle, Charlie Clark, and Michael Waye. Ralph and Gravelle have been living in Montreal, Edwards lives in Ganonoque, Clark moved to Saint John, N.B., in 1987, and Waye was last heard to be living in Burlington.

CLAIMS TO FAME:
Their biggest hit was "Stay Awhile", a million-seller written by singer Ken Tobias that hit #1 in Canada and was Top Ten in the U.S. Before that, they had success with "Moody Manitoba Morning" and "Fly Little White Dove, Fly". They appeared on The Tonight Show, The Merv Griffin Show, and a New Year's Eve TV special with fellow Canadian Guy Lombardo, broadcast throughout North America.

MUSICAL STYLE:
Soft, middle-of-the-road pop

WHERE ARE THEY NOW?
After leaving the Bells for a solo career, Edwards recorded a couple of albums and singles. He studied broadcasting, and was a set designer and cameraman for CKWS-TV in Kingston. He recorded a country-pop album in Nashville in 1988 and is now producing and writing a children's television show, "The Corner Store". He was also a sales representative for CFOX in Kingston. Ralph kept The Bells going until 1981, and has sung on commercials and jingles in Montreal, and has done fund-raising work. Gravelle has worked for a large retail firm, Clark did some jingles and studio work in Guelph before moving to Saint John, and Waye is still a musician. The Bells have done some reunion concerts in the past two years.

QUOTABLE QUOTE:
Ralph on The Bells' hits: "I still love to hear the songs. "Stay Awhile" is the song that I think I will be able to sing with my heart till the day I die."

FABULOUS FACT:
The Bells, who were having difficulty hitting the big time, were able to record "Stay Awhile," "Fly Little White Dove, Fly", and two other songs only because Edwards begged the outgoing president of Polydor Records for some studio time. According to Edwards, "the guy said 'what the heck, they can't fire me'," and approved the use of the studio. Although the song sounds tame by today's standards, "Stay Awhile" was banned by some Toronto radio stations for being too risqué.

Domenic Troiano: founder of The Mandala, now solo

trouble. I used to sleep in parked cars, a lot. Or slip into an office building at 9 o'clock before the maids left and locked me in there at night. Somewhere to sleep in November, you know? In the morning I'd go out and pick up some donuts at the restaurant where they'd just delivered them. I was a complete street kid. I was for a long time, right until I got into Yorkville.

I ended up in jail. I think it was up at Burwash that I knew this Indian kid named Fisher. I'll never forget this kid, 'cause he and his brothers were so poor they would set forest fires and then sign on to fight them. Now anybody who would want to fight a forest fire is really poor. And that's what they'd got busted for. You've got to be pretty desperate to do that, right? Anyway, when Fisher checked out, he left me this old Kay guitar. Up until then, I had wanted to play so bad that I got myself a book of chords and a cribbage board. And I drew the strings and frets on the cribbage board and I used to sing the notes, 'cause I knew what they were. I've got very good pitch. I've always had that. The Blood, Sweat & Tears horn section could tune to my voice. Bang, if I tell them that's the note, it's the note. And I think I developed that because for about three or four months there I would sit and fake out Presley tunes and "Laddy Miss Clauddy", and St. James Infirmary Blues, Muddy Waters stuff and try to fake it out the way I thought it would be on this cribbage board. And then this kid checked out and left me his Kay guitar — I guess he took pity on me — and within about six months I was playing in the Christmas concerts they had up there.

I found out very quickly that it was a way to avoid trouble. Nobody punched out the kid with the guitar. Especially the kid with the guitar who was on the boxing squad too. When I hit the street back in Toronto in the very early sixties, '62, I found, to my surprise, that the music that I'd been listening to before had hit Toronto in my absence. It was all over Yonge Street. There were bands like the Imperials. At Le Coq d'Or, every week, you'd see Muddy Waters, you'd see Bo Diddley, you'd see Motown bands up from Detroit. There was quite an active little scene. Our role models were downtown Yonge Street people like the Imperials with people like keyboard player Doug Riley. They were working. If they were doing it, why couldn't we do it?

That's all I thought of, every day that I was in jail, that I was going to get out and do that. I had finally found the first thing in my life that I was good at other than stealing donuts. I guess it all started with a bunch of the kids who were hanging around watching the Ronnie Hawkins band. I recruited a few of these guys and put a band together. We put together The Shays, the very first band on my own. By this time I was singing off and on with Ronnie. Most of them were kids from Downsview. Most of them were seven or eight years younger than me. They were still kids living at home; some of them were still in high school.

Eventually, The Shays got a hit with "Boom Boom" and "Walk That Walk" – back-to-back, two #1 hit records in Canada. For about six months we got a gig through Duff Roman, a disc jockey then, now with CHUM. Duff had a little club, an after hours club. After hours clubs were the big scene in Toronto then. The Imperial Club, the Bluenote. They were up and down Yonge Street. He tried to start one up on Davenport. It didn't last very long. He wasn't at the club the night we played first. But a lady named Sylvia Train was electrified and she called Duff on the phone and told him to get down here right away. So Duff came down and said he wanted to manage us.

We did a lot of heavy Chicago blues – Mississippi Delta Blues, Albert King – early, early Albert King, although nobody knew who he was then. And I started writing for the band. We did a bastardization of John Lee Hooker's "Boom Boom" called "Walk That Walk" which we considered a pretty safe bastardization because nobody in Toronto had ever heard "Boom Boom" at that point. It's become somewhat of a rock classic now. We went down to a little recording studio. Duff took us down. It cost us – it cost him – about 300 bucks and we recorded four sides. The first song out was "Boom Boom" and it went to #1 in about three weeks in Canada, nationwide. It was followed by "Walk That Walk" and "Out of the Sunshine".

Paul Anka had heard me do a gig in Ottawa. Paul was doing a television show out of New York called *Hullabaloo*, which was the East Coast equivalent of *The Shindig* that was on the West Coast at the time. He decided that they wanted to have a Canadian group on the show with Paul because, since Paul was the guest host that week, it would be appropriate to have a Canadian group; and by fluke we happened to have the #1 record in the country at the time, so they took us to New York.

We were in New York for three days to do the show and I wanted to live there. I heard more music in those three days than I'd heard in my entire life. Greenwich Village, the East Side, Trudy Heller's, the go-go bars uptown with Joey Dee and the Starlighters and stuff like that. Jazz like I'd never heard in my life before. Jazz to me was some kind of polite Appleyard stuff like I'd heard in Toronto. I'd never heard Jazz with fire and guts like that here. I went back to Toronto after the show and I was ruined. I was going back to New York. By hook or by crook. The Shays refused to go, so I left them.

I didn't manifest any anti-Canadian feelings whatsoever. I just knew where I wanted to go. Unfortunately, I feel that sometimes people in Canada tend to define everything in relation to how they feel about the United States. I prefer to live in the United States. So, what's wrong with Canada? Nothing is wrong with Canada. It's a wonderful place to live. I wish I could live there. In a lot of ways I wish I could have a home up in Toronto. I've tried a couple of times. But I make my career here in New York. This is where my fortune is. This is where my future is.

So, I went back and I heard music in New York that electrified me. The kids in Toronto were playing good strong rock 'n' roll but in New York it was on another level altogether. So I had a strange idea. I said I'll grab some Toronto guys and I'll form a New York type band. It'll be a fusion of jazz and rock. And the first person I went to was a jazz piano player named Tony Colacott. Brilliant young player, absolute idiot savant genius who played with Sarah Vaughan at age fourteen. I said "Let's get three guitar players and we'll orchestrate them like horns. Instead of strumming away, let's orchestrate them around the piano. And find a jazz-oriented bass player and drummer, and still keep it a rock band. We paid for a master ourselves. We went in and recorded "Brainwashed", which for 16 weeks was the #1 record in Canada. It blew everything off the charts – Beatles, Stones, everything. And it was my very first attempt at fusion music.

At that point I'd already started to leave the R&B field to a certain extent. Not to

David Clayton Thomas: the soul brother from Willowdale

BLAST

GENE CORNISH of The Rascals

BACKGROUND:
Ottawa-born Gene Cornish played guitar for The Rascals, the '60s rock and rhythm and blues group that was one of the most popular bands in North America. He moved to Rochester, N.Y. as a youngster when his mother – a former vocalist with Woody Herman and Ozzie Nelson – married an American. Cornish got hooked on the guitar when Elvis Presley moved rock 'n' roll to the forefront of popular music. Cornish met fellow Rascals Felix Cavaliere, Dino Danelli, and Eddie Brigati in New York City, where he now lives.

CLAIMS TO FAME:
Cornish got a break at the famed Peppermint Lounge where he played with Joey Dee and his Starlighters. Following that, he joined The Young Rascals (later The Rascals), and, through the mid to late '60s, the band notched a number of hit singles. Their first number one hit was "Good Lovin"; other chart classics included "Groovin", "A Girl Like You", "How Can I be Sure", "A Beautiful Morning", and "People Got To Be Free". The Rascals had nine *Top 20 songs in two years.*

MUSICAL STYLE:
Rock, ballads and R&B

WHERE IS HE NOW?:
Cornish left The Rascals in the early '70s, and later played with Bulldog, Fotomaker, and a local New York band, G.C. Dangerous. He and Danelli also produced April Wine's Live *album in the '70s. The Rascals reunited this spring and played the first leg of a reunion tour in the U.S. Northeast, Florida, and California. No Canadian dates were scheduled.*

QUOTABLE QUOTE:
The first reunion concert fell on Cornish's 44th birthday: "God, what a great present that was. I've had a lot of birthdays so far, and that's the best one I ever had... The performance went by so fast. It's like your first time having sex. You sort of remember it and you like it a lot, but 'Gee, could I do it again?' "

FABULOUS FACT:
After his stint with Joey Dee and His Starlighters, Cornish was approached by Cavaliere to form a new group. Cornish was reluctant to get involved and had to be talked into it by his parents and some girlfriends. He went back to New York and joined what became The Rascals. He says that the first time the group got together in Cavaliere's basement "changed my life. We hit magic at that rehearsal."

leave it, but I thought to expand on it. I remember walking down Yorkville and I heard something coming out of a store window and it was the guitar solo on "Taxman" from Rubber Soul. It stopped me dead in my tracks. It was very similar to what we were doing, similar to "Brainwashed" with its orchestration of guitars. This was what I was aspiring to.

We could not get a US deal for "Brainwashed". Duff tried every way he could. It was an anti-Vietnam war song, basically, which was not a popular issue in the United States in 1963. Radio stations just wouldn't take a chance on stuff like that. But we still had the #1 record in Canada so we decided that we were going to try to be the band which did the first coast-to-coast Canadian tour. Nobody had ever tried it and we decided to make it a motorized tour – certainly the money wasn't there to fly. We got together with Ronnie Scribner, an agent out of Toronto, and he put together a coast-to-coast tour which turned out to be a total disaster. We just thought we'd buy a truck and start driving.

We had dates booked all the way from Toronto up through to Orillia up to North Bay, over the Sault, Thunder Bay, Kirkland Lake – and right out west to Edmonton and Vancouver. We were going to appear at Klondike Days – it all looked good on paper. So away we went: I've got three kid guitar players who've never been away from home before in their lives. I've got a junkie piano player who's a walking pharmacy. We get about three gigs under our belt and we pull into Sault Saint Marie, Ontario. In the middle of this gig in the local hockey arena, a motorcycle gang from Sault Saint Marie, Michigan invaded the dance. Bad, tough Indian kids from the North. One hellacious brawl broke out in the audience right in the middle of our show. And it boiled up and got onto the stage. Microphones started going down and amps started getting broken. Tony Colacott, who's a very frail little guy, got sucker-punched by some guy who was three times his size, knocked him stone cold. The manager's office was in the back and the manager had a 12-gauge standing beside his desk – and I knew it was there because we'd been in there to get paid earlier. Amps were getting broken, my band was going down under this wave of people, it was really getting life-threatening – so I ran back to

Joni Mitchell: from folk to jazz-inflected musings

the manager's office and I grabbed his 12-gauge, checked to see if it was loaded, ran out to centre stage and put two rounds through the ceiling of the arena, and stopped the fight in a big hurry. When the smoke cleared, the place was empty. They were gone. Ever hear a shotgun go off in a metal arena? I couldn't hear for two days.

We loaded all our broken equipment into the truck and took off out of town, north of

BLAST

THE DE FRANCO FAMILY

BACKGROUND:
Band members were Tony (b.Aug.31, 1959), Benny (b. July 11, 1954), Marisa (b. July 23, 1955), Nino (b. Oct. 19, 1956) and Merlina De Franco (b.July 20, 1957). They came from the Niagara Peninsula community of Port Colborne. All are now married and live in southern California.

CLAIMS TO FAME:
The Canadian answer to The Osmonds, their biggest hit was "Heartbeat – It's A Lovebeat", a song that hit #1 throughout North America in 1973. They followed it up with the million-seller "Abracadabra". During the early '70s, the De Francos could be seen on most major TV variety shows.

MUSICAL STYLE:
Pop, bubblegum

WHERE ARE THEY NOW?
The De Francos stopped performing in 1979, and, though they live near Los Angeles, they're leading "normal lives". Tony, the former heart-throb of the group, runs a production company with his wife. The couple co-ordinates recording projects and produces various performers from around the world. Tony hopes to begin recording again, and is considering writing a book on the group's exploits. Benny is a film producer at Walt Disney studios. Nino manages a music store in the San Fernando Valley. Marisa and Merlina are housewives.

QUOTABLE QUOTE:
Tony, on the chances of returning to Canada: "We're a long way from Port Colborne. I really love Canada, but I've been here since I was 13. I almost don't feel Canadian anymore. But don't get me wrong. I don't feel I've abandoned Canada. Besides, we're all still Canadian citizens.

FABULOUS FACT:
The De Francos were so popular in their heyday that a quick read of any of the teen magazines of the era reveals their birthdates, hair and eye colour, and hobbies. Tony, for example, loved "hockey, go-carting, and eating ice cream".

Neil Young: unrepentent rocker

the Sault, heading toward Thunder Bay. Between the Sault and Thunder Bay, there's about 600 miles of nothing. We get about five miles out of town and see headlights behind us. It's the motorcycle gang from Michigan: they're following us out of town. Now, I had stolen the shotgun. When we threw the equipment into the back of the truck, I literally threw the shotgun in, too. So I'm squatted behind the Fender amplifier in their headlights with the 12-gauge on top of the amp. They fell back. The guitar player, the kid that was driving, got so scared that he got about another 10 miles down the road and drove the truck off the road. I mean, clean off the road, turned it right over. Me, the shotgun and the amplifier went the length of the truck and right out through the front window. Smashed the radiator and totalled the truck. This was a big step-over van that I'd bought for the trip for about $300. So there we are, maybe 200 miles out of the city, in a ditch, at 3 o'clock in the morning. There's nobody out there. We sat shivering in the van all night and we set out walking in the morning and found a house about two or three miles down the road. We had some money — we had picked up three gigs already, so we had a couple of grand with us — and we got a taxi to come and take us to the city with a taxi and a U-Haul.

In the city, another disaster developed. Word had gotten back to Toronto of what had happened and Ron Scribner decided he was going to cancel the tour. So he called ahead to all the other gigs and told them we weren't coming. So we were stuck in the middle. We didn't have money to get home; we didn't have money to get out. But Duff knew a radio disc jockey in Edmonton who was promoting the Klondike Days fair. Duff called ahead and said that we could save one gig — the Edmonton gig — which was the big one. He was a saint of a disc jockey. I believe it was Duff's younger brother. He spoke to the promoters and saved our gig. We played a solid week in Edmonton — a very successful week.

But that was about it for me. If that was what touring in Canada was like... So I came back off that tour and within a matter of days, John Lee Hooker was playing in Yorkville, and I used to go down and sit in with him — back him up, play guitar. John told

John Kay and Steppenwolf: up from Yorkville

me he was opening in the Cafe A Go-Go in the Village the following Monday and did I want to come with him? I would do guitar and I would sing backup. And I fell in with John because of "Boom Boom". He'd heard my recording and we became friends.

Besides, John, who is, for the most part, illiterate, doesn't have a driver's license. He had had some chick travelling with him who had been his driver. She had disappeared. As a matter of fact, I think she disappeared with his car. So John said: "You can drive to New York."

When Blood, Sweat and Tears finally came together, we had a reputation as being musically and personally a renegade band. Nobody was doing anything like what we were doing. The bands that were being successful were playing what people wanted to. We were a complete outlaw band; jazz musicians didn't know what to make of us. We really didn't have a niche. We were street kids.

We worked all the little clubs up and down Yorkville. I'd be playing at the Patio. Joni Mitchell would be at the Gaslight. Tony Colacott would be at the Penny Farthing. Neil Young used to play at the Penny Farthing. The Purple Onion. On that block, where all those boutiques are now, there had to be about 10 or 15 clubs in that two-block stretch between Avenue Road and Bay Street.

Joni interested me very much because I heard Joni doing things melodically that were head and shoulders above anything that I was hearing around. Maybe I shouldn't put it on such a competitive basis, but what I heard from Joni was, again, jazz. Something there – what I had heard in New York. She was just a tremendously inventive singer.

Although she didn't know it and probably doesn't know it till this day, I was madly in love with Joni Mitchell for about a year and I kind of moped around the clubs and watched her and admired her from afar. I was overwhelmed by her, very much so, in those days. She was an extraordinarily beautiful girl, she's still a very attractive woman. But Joni was, in those years, maybe 19, 20, 21. She was a stunner – voice like an angel.

For a while I went under the name of Sonny Thomas. My birth name is Thomset. That name has had a criminal record with it. Every time some cop pulled over this hippie on Yorkville, it was over to 52 Division to get my ass kicked. Run me up on their little checklist, take one look at my record and kick my ass in a minute.

So believe me, I was really circumspect in those days. I was making a living being a musician. Hell, I didn't need a break & entry. The furthest thing from my mind was going back to jail. I'd be the last person on Yorkville to break into anything at that point. 'Cause I knew what was waiting for me. So I changed my name to Sonny Thomas and there was a big black dude, who sang the blues, named Stan Thomas. Stan also took the name Sonny Thomas. So we had a big argument about who was going to be Sonny Thomas. Stan, being big, about 6 foot 4, a tall black dude – well, I really didn't want to tangle with him. I said, "Okay, you can be Sonny Thomas. I'll be David Clayton Thomas, how's that?" Stan and I went on to be great friends. We were friends for quite a long time.

I used to see a lot of Ricky James, too. Ricky had a house band at the Purple Onion on Avenue Road. Remember, these bands used to go and sit in with each other, too. Between sets and after hours or off nights, you'd find John Kay, later of Steppenwolf, sitting in with my band.

In the end, we all split at the same time – Joni, Neil, myself. Joni and Neil to California, myself and a few other people went to New York. I guess we made a fair amount of impact. There was no colour bar here and there was a colour bar very strongly enforced in the United States. We had mixed bands in Canada. But we could never play in Detroit. The agents would tell us, "You come down here with a white band or you come down with a black band – one or the other."

BLAST

FIVE MAN ELECTRICAL BAND

BACKGROUND:
First known as the Staccatos, the group came together in Ottawa in 1963, headed by local DJ Dean Hagopian, with Brian Rading on bass, Les Emmerson and Vern Craig on guitars and drummer Rick Belanger. Hagopian and Craig later left, and drummer Mike Belanger (Rick's brother) and keyboard player Ted Gerow joined. In 1969, the name was changed to The Five Man Electrical Band. Some early difficulties put the band on the verge of breaking up. They were in the middle of a softball game in Ottawa when they got word that one of their singles was on its way up the chart. The group set up base in Los Angeles, and enjoyed great popular success until it folded in 1972-73.

CLAIMS TO FAME:
The band cut six LPs and a stack of 45s, including "Half Past Midnight", "Moonshine", "Werewolf", "I'm A Stranger Here", and "Abso– lutely Right". Their biggest hit was "Signs", (the song they heard about at the softball game), which sold 1.5 million copies, and became a North American anti-establishment anthem and went Top five in the US. Their other singles did well on North American charts. The band played for the Queen in Ottawa in 1967.

MUSICAL STYLE:
Rock-and-roll with strong vocals and a hint of country

WHERE ARE THEY NOW?:
After the band split, Emmerson stayed in L.A., where he released singles "Control Of Me" and "Cry Your Eyes Out". He now lives in Ottawa where he's a partner in a music production company. Gerow was US singer Bobby Vee's music director before settling in Ottawa as a freelance record producer, working with artists such as Canadian Carroll Baker. Rading renovates houses and plays with town local groups in Ottawa. Rick Belanger went solo in L.A., with little success, and now installs computer cable systems in Toronto. Mike Belanger played with an Ottawa band for 14 years before joining a courier company. The Five Man Electrical Band reunited in 1986 and has since played a number of Ontario concerts.

QUOTABLE QUOTE:
Emmerson on writing of "Signs": "We were driving along a highway in the US and there were advertising signs everywhere. I thought, "What a shame to cover up this lovely country' ".

FABULOUS FACT:
It was their lack of US success that led the band to almost split in 1971. "Signs", which was earlier released almost unnoticed by Bobby Vee and as flip side of another Five Man record, changed all that, making the band one of Canada's most popular in the early '70s.

Mixed bands could not work in the U.S. So Toronto became a very important stop for the black artists who could come up and work main room clubs out of the U.S. We were exposed to the Temptations and Ben E. King and Muddy and Bo Diddley. In Toronto, they played up and down the strip constantly. It was a breeding ground, a training ground for the young Canadian musicians. Not too many people in the United States realized at the time that The Band was Canadian. They thought that it was an Arkansas blues band. As we all know, they're from Kitchener, Ontario.

But me, I was not trying to push into Canada, I was pushing out of Canada — closer to the music that I wanted to play coming out of Detroit and Buffalo. I didn't really know too much about the United States except that the music that I wanted to play was being played at its best in the United States. I think a lot of us felt that way. So we all left, and the City of Toronto, in its ultimate wisdom, decided to clean up Yorkville. Cleaning it up meant, first of all, driving those scruffy rock musicians out of there, putting some fashionable boutiques in, and raising the rents.

Ex-leader of The Shays and Blood, Sweat and Tears, David Clayton Thomas now makes his home in New York.

2
POMPADOURS & CIRCUMSTANCE

by Carole Pope

Carole Pope and Kevin Staples: victims of fashion

ife imitates art: The fashion system spits out tens of thousands of clones, all effecting style like camouflage. Everyday, we come face to face with Michael Jacksons, George Michaels, Springsteens, and Madonnas. Youth wrapped in the fetishism of their idols. The rock'n'roll uniform: white T-shirt, blue jeans, and black leather jacket become the street idiom. What about Canada, wedged between American and British rock culture? How did our sense of style evolve?

Canadian rock 'n' roll was spawned in the 50s, somewhere between Giselle MacKenzie and Juliette. It began with the boy groups, milquetoast in Brooks Brothers suits, crooning cutesy songs to teens and housewives. Who could ever forget the four Lads, the Crew Cuts, and the Diamonds? Then came Canada's first rock rebel: Ronnie Hawkins, the guy your mom didn't want you to date. He was hipness dressed up in a sharkskin suit. He was dangerous. He had gone to first base — and beyond. He was arrogant and cool. He'd been used by a woman and was here to sing about it.

After the earth-shattering event of the emasculated Elvis returning home from serving his country, a new non-threatening white-bread male came into vogue: "The Bobby Syndrome". A barrage of Bobbys, and Bobby types descended on us like a plague — Bobby Rydell, Bobby Vee, Frankie Avalon, Fabian, Tommy Sands, and Bobby Darin. Canada's contribution to this malaise 'o' Bobbys was Bobby Curtola. He was too cute and cuddly for words. He dressed in cashmere sweaters, baby blue sequins, and sported a tartan tux jacket. His blonde hair was styled in a conservative pompadour.

But Bobby's days were numbered. Direct from the streets and dance clubs of Toronto, a phenomenon appeared. It was called the "Toronto Sound". Steamy, soulful R&B music served up by white boys. Some great bands came out of those days in the early '60s: Roy Kenner and the Associates, The Rogues,

Bobby Curtola: cashmere sweaters and baby blues

Teenage Head: punk attitude to burn

(later to become the Mandala), Robbie Lane and the Disciples, Jon and Lee and the Checkmates, who would metamorphosize into Rhinoceros. And there were great vocalists such as Dianne Brooks, Shirley Matthews, and gender bender Jackie Shane. These performers came on cool and urbane in iridescent mohair suits, tab collar shirts, stove pipe pants, and cuban heeled shoes. Their cologne? *Brute*. Fans would quote every line from the *James Brown Live at the Appolo* album. It was all part of the "negro assimilation look".

In the middle '60s, with the advent of the British invasion, London was in. It became the vortex of creation. The excesses of the '60s were magnified in the clothing. The redefinition of lifestyle and fashion was influenced by pop groups. With it came sexual liberation, and to some extent, women's liberation. Fashion and music catered to the youth cult. Canadians assimilated British and American Pop Culture and spewed it out, redefined by our own sensibilities.

Canadian bands of the '60s each cultivated their own style. Toronto's Ugly Ducklings were known as the Stone clones; they had the bad boy look. Their sound was a hybrid of British bands and their own original music. The Kensington Market was the first Canadian band to incorporate a synthesizer into music. They wore sex-defining blue jeans, and a drug crazed look in their eyes. Montreal's Influence had two lead guitarists. Their late singer, Bo Bo Island, wore a leather jacket, a pencil-thin mustache, and greased back hair. The Paupers and Steppenwolf affected world-weary attitudes; the Stormy Clovers were a study in terminal coolness. Yorkville's bands sported Union Jack jackets, florescent body paint, paisley and floral print shirts, capes, evil black boots, and conveyed more with a toss of their pampered, flowing hair than words can define.

Murray McLauchlan: salute to a city kid

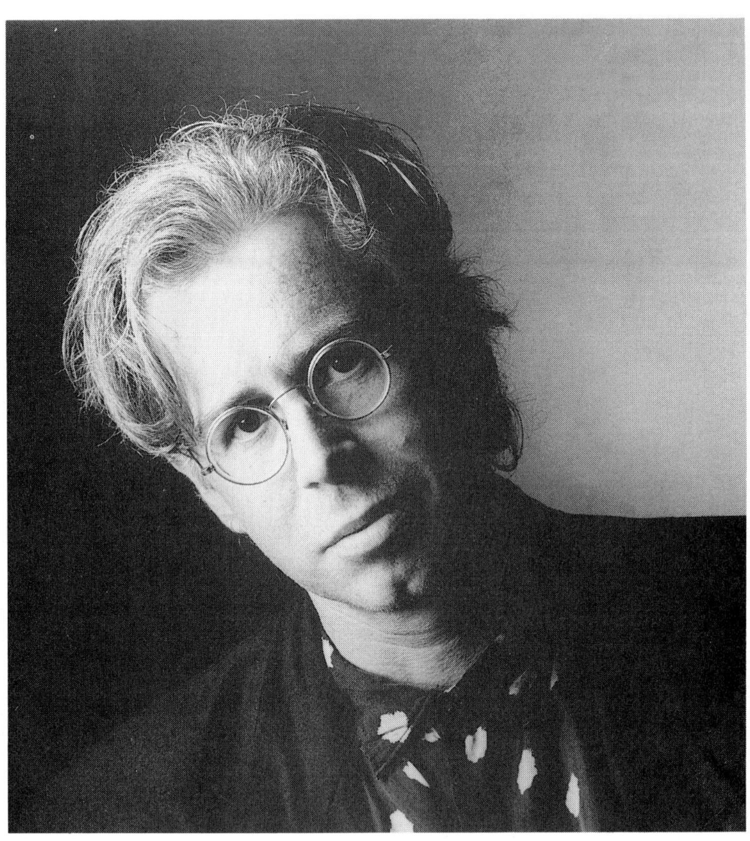

Bruce Cockburn: music that makes a difference

Western Canada, not to be outdone, gave us The Guess Who. The young Burton Cummings, their singer, had Jim Morrison-like Charisma. The Stampeders and Bachman Turner Overdrive (forerunners of the fatboy look so prevalent in today's Canadian bands), also hailed from the west. Buffy Ste. Marie did the native Indian thing, with a bad case of vibrato. Leonard Cohen, Canada's rock poet laureate, was the forerunner of a look that still makes a statement today: basic black. Murray McLauchlan did the cowboy, folky thing, and Joni Mitchell gave us angst in a caftan.

Clubs of the '60s featured psychedelic light shows, with go-go dancers. Bands and audiences alike escaped into fantasy and hedonist, drug-induced self-expression and role-playing.

With the death throes of the '60s the '70s, the new and frightening "Me Decade", dawned upon us. It brought with it Glam Rock, and its sister-in-sin disco. Glam assaulted our senses with pimpish, theatrical glamour. It gave males a chance to flaunt bisexuality, and introduced us to the world of spandex, platform shoes, and shag hairdos. Canadian purveyors of Glam include Moxy, Fludd, Rhinegold (from which Gowan emerged), Max Webster, and Brutus, whose lead singer, Walter Zwol, had a shaved head.

When it came to disco, Gino Vannelli gave us the ultimate in pimp playboy style, coupled with ludicrous male posturing. He wore flowing silk scarves, and was obsessed with exposing his hairy chest. Fortunately, his music more than compensated for his lack of taste. Others who embraced the shlock/glamour of the disco era were Rick James, Claudja Barry, the Raes, Patsy Gallant, and Lisa Dal Bello.

Just when everyone was experiencing the dry heaves from '70s music, an underground phenomena breathed life into the stagnant music scene. Bands such as the Sex Pistols,

Platinum Blonde: teen idols to metal poseurs

The Guess Who: a gift from the West

Talking Heads, Blondie, and Rough Trade were breaking new musical ground. A gritty, stark urban style of writing and performing tore through all the vacuous noise that polluted the airwaves and dance clubs. Punk and New Wave was born.

It was much more than music: it was an upheaval in art, fashion, and lifestyle. Many British bands broke in Canada first; and Toronto responded with a wealth of its own innovative bands. My band, Rough Trade, love it or hate it, was responsible for blowing the scene wide open. We were involved in creating not just music, but themes for each performance. We became slaves of fashion. We were so repulsed by the slovenly look of most bands that we resolved to bring some semblance of theatre into our act. Some of the transformations we went through were

BLAST

FLUDD

BACKGROUND:
In the early '70s, Toronto band Fludd cornered the outrageous market in Canadian rock music with their wild stage antics and glitter makeup. A saying in Toronto music circles in the early '70s was "Lighthouse plays for peace; Fludd plays for chicks." Original Fludd members were Brian and Ed Pilling (who were originally from Birmingham, England), Greg Godovitz, Peter Csankey, and John Anderson. Gord Wasczek also played for the band.

CLAIMS TO FAME:
Despite their image, Fludd members were also talented musicians who hit the charts with successful singles such as "Turned 21", "What An Animal", "Brother and Me", and "Cousin Mary". They also released a couple of albums. Before forming Fludd, the Pilling brothers had played in a band, The Wages of Sin, and backed Cat Stevens.

MUSICAL STYLE:
Popular rock

WHERE ARE THEY NOW?:
The band broke up when Brian Pilling died of cancer. His brother, Ed, has worked at a number of jobs, including running a fish and chips wagon. He has been involved recently in renovating and rebuilding houses. He lives in Pickering and still performs occasionally. Godovitz formed his own successful group, Goddo, which disbanded in 1987. Goddo is planning a return to the stage in 1989. Godovitz has written a number of new songs and has performed on occasion. Csankey owns an electronics company in Toronto, and Anderson plays drums for Corey Hart. Wasczek was in successful rock band Leigh Ashford before joining Fludd. He's been involved in the Toronto music scene throughout the '80s, and plays with former Sweet Blindness vocalist Bobby Dupont.

QUOTABLE QUOTE:
Ed Pilling: "Fludd gave some class to the Canadian music industry by taking things a little bit farther than where they were, dressing it up a bit. I think we gave a lot of fun to it, too. We always had fun, and I think people knew that."

FABULOUS FACT:
As a mock protest to what the band believed was too much interference by their record company and distributors, the guys in Fludd posed nude for the music magazine Rainbow. *The picture also turned up in the promo packages accompanying the official release of the album.*

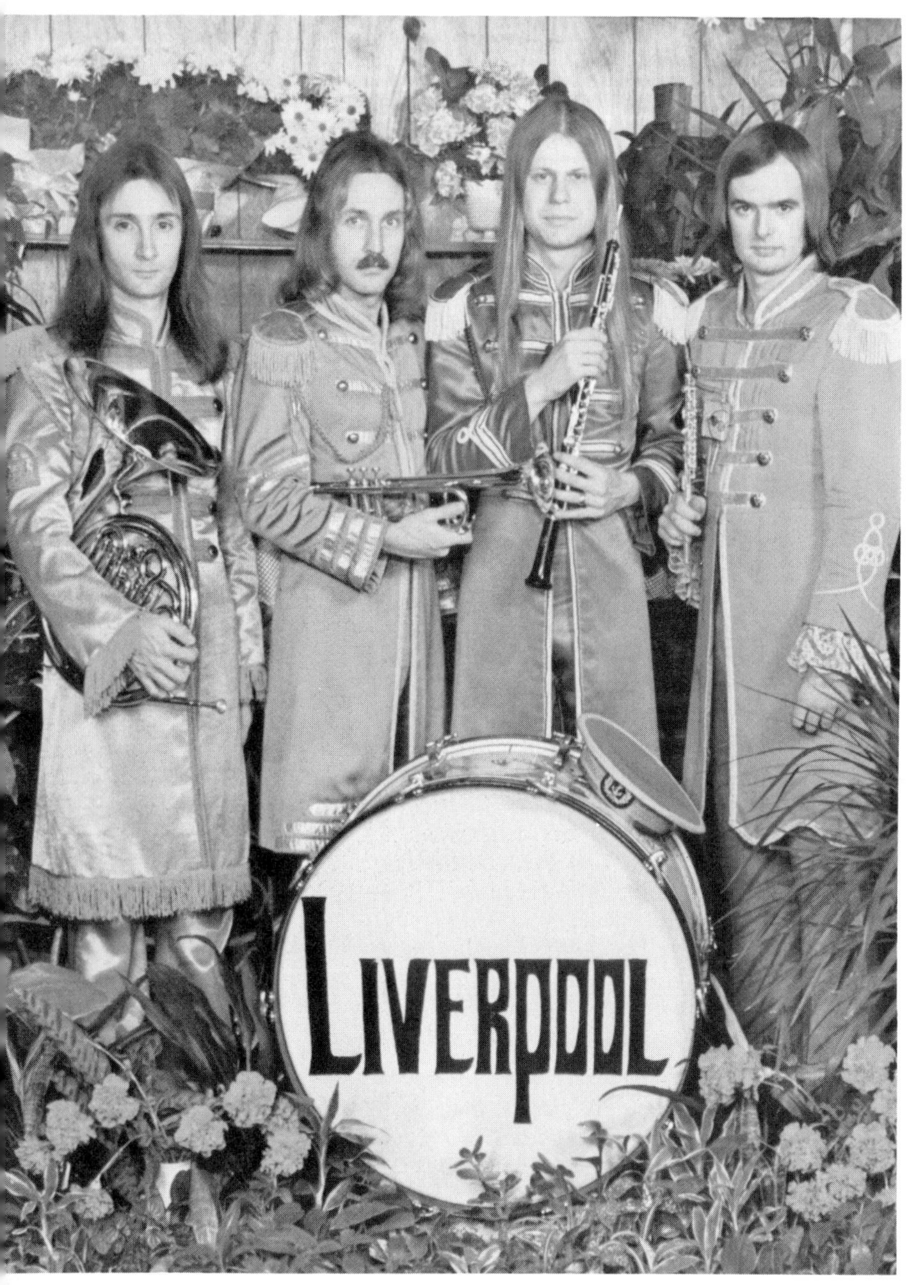

Liverpool: imitation as the sincerest form of flattery

"I can't remember the chords and I can't remember the lyrics" (the frightened animal look), the *ceŕe* (polyester to you) jumpsuit (just an excuse to expose a lot of skin), and my favourite, the evil black bondage suit. We wore clothes by designers such as Vivienne Westwood, Toronto's Marilyn Kiewiet and Sandy Stagg, and the orgasmic leathers of Claude Montana. All the bands that followed us had distinctly different styles of music and image. They included Drastic Measures, The Dishes (who can ever forget their song "Richard Speck with a Philipino nurse by the Neck"), The Vile Tones (whose singer Nazi Dog was heavily into bloodletting on stage), the Diodes, The Curse (they gave a whole new meaning to tampons), The B-Girls, (who had a fabulous image and were great musicians), Martha and the Muffins, Teenage Head (they wrote the book on attitude), The Government, and the Battered Wives.

As the '70s moved into the '80s, Canadian artists developed their own distinct identities. They were much more self-assured as performers and artists. With the advent of videos, bands became Video directors; costume designers, and makeup artists all contributed to what a band wanted to project. Some bands maintained total artistic control, while others fell prey to the whims and demands of record companies, and video directors. Many bands used sensationalism, such as sex and violence, to beef up a weak image.

On the other hand, there was Bryan Adams. His music is uncomplicated, passionate rock 'n' roll; his trademark, the white T-shirt. His image typifies the Canadian male: the down-home boy with a guitar, singing about love and pain. In contrast, Gowan projects an ethereal image with his clothes and body language, which probably appeals more to women. Much of his work is too incisive and well-crafted to be appreciated by the masses.

The Diodes: punk rock rebels ▶

Colin James: roots guitar rock from the West

Corey Hart's image is an '80s version of James Dean: the pout, the grainy video footage, reminiscent of old photographs of Dean. Nash the Slash is one artist who defies notoriety by bandaging his head like the invisible man. Dal Bello cultivates an anti-fashion, anti-taste image. The Parachute Club utilizes an ethno beat, coupled with African

Lisa Dal Bello: shock-rock chanteuse

The Parachute Club: Queen Street West revolutionary chic

dance movements. Their look is somewhere between terrorist chic and urban guerrilla, with a touch of PLO thrown in for good measure. Bruce Cockburn is an artist who lives the lifestyle of an urban guerrilla. He not only writes and performs brilliant thought-provoking music, he travels to political hot spots and experiences first-hand the social injustices and discontent, which he then incorporates into his art.

Jane Siberry, the high priestess of new age music, is one of the few Canadian artists who utilizes performance art in every aspect of her work. She is in a state of constant change; therefore she is always evolving as an artist. But when it comes to the strongest and most identifiable persona, no one can top k.d. lang. She's a combination of Annie Oakley, six guns blazing, and Betty Hutton

Buffy Ste. Marie: back to the land and native roots

in the film *Annie Get Your Gun*. She uses comedy and charisma. She has introduced a whole new genre to country music: The Western Torch Singer. The most recent performers to come out of Canada have reverted to the anti-image image. Blue Rodeo, Spirit of the West, and Andrew Cash have no discernible difference in their appearance. They're heavily into denim. These artists are more concerned with making music than projecting an image, which in itself is not a bad thing. Whether we like it or not, we have created a monster, and because the market is glutted with performers, an artist is doomed unless he or she has some semblance of an image.

Carole Pope founded Rough Trade in the mid-1970s with partner Kevin Staples. She is now recording a new solo album and completing a screenplay for CBC-Television.

3

THE RISE AND FALL (AND RISE AGAIN) OF FRENCH POP

by John Griffen

Luba: Ukranian folkie turned pop star

Round up a gang of the old Quebeçois cultural guard. Plant them in the Montreal bistro of their choice and keep the bar open until sentimental hour. Check back in sometime between five and fist fights and you'll find them propping each other up and holding back the tears as they confess that, yes, Felix Leclerc is the founder of Quebec pop music and the father of us all.

It's a neat conceit — that Leclerc, the folk singer-poet who put Quebec on the international musical map; who had *tout le Paris* flocking to his shows in the early '50s; who influenced a generation of artists at home and abroad — should be considered the author of our popular identity and source of our great national pride. And especially now, after he died at the age of 74 in August 1988, with his memory enshrined in the hearts of millions, and his name affixed to our version of the Canadian entertainment industry Junos — the Felix awards — and slapped on road signs around the province.

Yeah, it's a nice conceit all right. Too bad it's not true. For all his far-reaching influence and enduring legend, Leclerc wouldn't have recognized rock 'n' roll if it had come up and bussed him on both cheeks. Literate, sensitive, reflective — he had all those qualities and more, but everybody knows they add up to diddly squat in the lexicon of rock.

You want to find out where the devil's music was really spawned in Quebec? You have to let yourself free-float back to early 1969. That's not so hard; it was a pretty good year for music everywhere. But try wrapping your head around this one for a moment. We're in the countryside a couple of hours east of Montreal. Actually, we're in a country club, one of those places with the manicured golf courses and the wood-tone bars, where the favourite colour is plaid, and people's idea of dressing for dinner means putting on violent red blazers, ordering drinks with umbrellas in them, and hoping

Robert Charlebois: agent provocateur

that maybe Paul Anka will be providing the tunes for your wining 'n' dining entertainment tonight. Into this happy and secure scenario, where baldness and blue rinse are the coifs of choice, lurches something they have not envisioned in their *cauchemars*. And, if they have, it has always involved their children and bike gangs, rape, pillage, plunder, and the destruction of the establishment order. Into this scenario lurches Robert Charlebois.

You don't know it's Robert Charlebois, not really, and not right away, because whatever is screaming into the microphone right now is wearing a lone ranger mask, a red sequined Canadiens hockey sweater, and silver "glam" bell-bottoms so dazzling you're screaming for your shades.

And who the hell is that behind him? This masked man and his electrified mountain of hair are not alone. There are 10, maybe 15, freaks in this band, wailing away on guitars and horns and drums and percussion, and setting up a noise to uncurl the sets on the folks sitting stunned and sonically flash-frozen to their plushy upholstered supper club seats.

Wilder yet, the guy is singing in French, and not France French from Paris, the language of traditional *chansonniers* and the snooty international passkey to acceptance in Francophone culture. No, he's howling his brains out in *joual*, the local jargon of the working stiff, known to everyone and generally understood to be something you send your kids to school to unlearn. Somehow, though, it fits here, against the raging backbeat, the progressive jazz-fills, and the firebomb guitars — almost as though the will of the people has suddenly been expressed through the absurdly simple, sweaty coupling of street lingo and rock 'n' roll.

But here's the truly absurd thing: by the time the night is over, by the time Charlebois has worked the room, developed his Joe "Fingers" Ledoux everyman alter ego and sung his hit "Lindbergh!!!" with Louise Forrestier wailing like a five-alarm siren behind him, by the time he's done all his rock 'n' roller can do to survive in a strange room, the crowd is on its feet, shouting and waving and asking for more.

That's right. Those who haven't run for shelter with the first wave of aural abuse have fallen hook, line, and heart attack for a 24-year-old *"gars bien ordinaire"* from Montreal named Robert Charlebois and his vision of *Quebeçois* rock 'n' roll. By the end of 1969, they would have plenty of company.

* * *

Before Charlebois, the whole rock thing in this province had been a joke, a novelty item. There'd been Les Classels, guys who dyed their hair white, wore white clothes, and played Merseybeat covers. Or J.B. And The Playboys, a band that had Beatle wigs for awhile and actually wrote some good tunes before self-destructing. And, for a brief hallucinatory period in Montreal, there'd been a flash fire of psychedelic activity that saw great bands such as the Haunted, the Rabble, and Sidetrack flair up, only to crash and burn in the solar activity of the time.

Offenbach: progressive rock with symphonic scope

But Charlebois put the whole thing into perspective — if that's what you call his initial anarcho/joyful "fuck you" attitude to everything. At the same time, he wrote songs that spoke savagely and tenderly to the very soul of a generation raised second-hand on the music of Britain and the U.S.

He was the first to fine-tune the unique situation of being a French island in a sea of English; a fragile, vibrant culture tied on the one hand to France and Europe, and on the other, bound to the brash, trash commercialism and open—highway fantasies of the States. What Charlebois — what the province-wide anthem "Lindbergh!!!" — accomplished was nothing more or less than the mobilization of an entire young mob bent on making rock 'n' roll *de chez nous*.

Charlebois himself went on to many things, not all of which had much to do with rock. He's had his share of successes here and in France, his share of setbacks, and his share of comebacks, too. But, however he's judged come the final great day, one thing is sure: he opened the whole sorry floodgates for what's sluiced through the chutes since then.

And there's been a ton of it. Consider if you will a country of 6 million, bombarded on all sides save the Arctic Ocean by the seductive lure of the States and all that that entails. Then understand that Quebec currently has a multi-million dollar entertainment industry that employs thousands at every level from gofer to record company president; supports dozens of recording studios, radio and TV stations; feeds gossip to teen mags and fanzines; finds work for live clubs, discos, and deejays; has a 24-hour rock video cable network, and the rest of the infrastructure that props up the mega-billion music biz in Canada, the US, and Europe.

What happened here parallels what happened everywhere else; it just doesn't always seem that way to outsiders. What Elvis and The Beatles and The Stones and the flower power thing did to an outdated, moribund industry elsewhere, they did here in lesser numbers. Plus, there had always been a homegrown market for cover tunes, in which Quebec singers would take versions of international hits, slap French lyrics on the melodies, re-record them, and put them out for the local market.

Still, BC — "before Charlebois" — you're right. Generally speaking, it was always a colonialist kind of thing, with the pop culture being created elsewhere, pressed elsewhere, and shipped here for consumption, with most of the profits being shipped right back out again.

That changed with Charlebois — and this is absolutely the last time his name will come up in present company. Suddenly, there were new bands, new singers, all wanting to play pop, sing in French, and *do it all here*. And of these, the most overwhelmingly successful was Beau Dommage.

Here was a prime cut, grade A example of the great Quebec-America mutant synthesis at work. The five men and women who became the province's supergroup for the '70s were children of the '60s: raised on pop, educated through the new junior college system here, and fully aware of the new wave of nationalism sweeping over Quebec.

Harmonium's Serge Fiori and Louis Valois

Ginette Reno: a voice in search of an image

After giggling in parents' basements, playing rooms such as the late great Hotel Nelson in Old Montreal, and sucking up sources like sponges, Beau Dommage released a debut self-titled LP that hit the streets Dec. 9, 1974. It sold 5,000 copies in the first week of release, 50,000 by Christmas that year, and has since found a place in a staggering 350,000 homes from Senneville to Senneterre.

The music was lovely – soft, slightly countrified pop with an urban Quebeçois perspective, and sweet harmonies that owed no little to the work of Crosby, Stills and Nash. But their immediate acceptance was a question of being in the right place at the right time, a question of finding and supporting the Quebeçois psyche in its most vulnerable formative stages.

In hindsight, their success meshed nicely with the rise of the Parti Quebeçois to political power, when people were searching for an identity that wasn't French, that wasn't Canadian, that wasn't American – and yet was all of these things. Beau Dommage helped provide the Quebeçois with a new identity.

Although Beau Dommage never again hit with the ferocity of that initial impact, they released three more best-selling records, did boffo box office on tour, and effectively reigned as the band to beat, before retiring gracefully in 1978. Their influence remains pervasive, both in the substantial current solo careers of ex-band members Michel Rivard, Pierre Bertrand, and Marie-Michelle Desrosiers, and as a result of three massive reunion concerts before 60,000 people in Montreal and Quebec City in 1974.

Beau Dommage was not the only band, however, to anticipate, reflect or take advantage of the patriotic, independent spirit that was Quebec through the '70s. Their biggest rivals were Harmonium, a peace-and-love folk/jazz/rock ensemble led by Serge Fiori

Cano: folk rock à la français

Felix Leclerc: the patron saint of Quebec pop

that sold hundreds of thousands of albums after their incredible debut in 1974.

Philosophically speaking, Harmonium was a light-weight version of what hadn't been all that heavy to begin with. But they snared the Quebeçois passion for British progressive rock bands such as Yes, Genesis, and Supertramp by incorporating arty keyboards and creating mini-orchestral works for their fans' delighted consumption. The band made in-roads in Toronto, and even played that mecca of Quebec rock 'n' roll, California; but, they ran out of gas just short of their breakthrough destination. Only Serge Fiori would rise again in a solo career.

There were no others to truly take their place, although plenty in the '70s were willing to try. Gilles Vigneault became, simply, the social conscience of Quebec, and his song *"Gens du Pays"* its national anthem, while singers such as Claude Dubois and Jean-Pierre Ferland built and maintained strong solo careers by melding the French *chansonnier* tradition with progressive musical arrangements, distinctive Quebec perspectives, and, in the case of Dubois, a rock 'n' roll outlaw attitude.

His outrageous female counterpart was singer Diane Dufresne, who posed for her first poster wearing nothing on her chest but a body-painted Quebec flag, and whose flamboyant statements, lifestyle, and concerts fuelled the province's gossip rags for years — even after Dufresne had abandoned the bright lights of Montreal for the brighter lights of L.A. and Paris.

In that, she bucked a trend by Quebec artists to hitch their stars to one of two prevailing American musical styles in the '70s. Bands such as Barde, the Francophone Ontario-based Cano, Les Seguins, and vastly underrated interstellar duo Fraser and DuBolt, picked up on the folk-based, back-to-the-land mindset of The Band, Dylan, and the Grateful Dead. Others such as Ginette

Michel Pagliaro: once and future king of French rock

Reno and the young Rene Simard went Hollywood, using big arrangements and bigger bands to establish mainstream audiences here and across the country. If ever a pop stylist deserved a break in the US and elsewhere, it has been Reno – she could sing a recipe to emotional mush – but it hasn't really happened. At least, not yet.

Lost in all this positive motivation toward folk, or social statement, or pop or progressive rock, during the '70s was the voice of the pure rock 'n' roller. The great Ville Emard Blues Band, despite its epocal headlining concert at the Montreal Canadiens shrine, the Forum, was essentially a one-off supergroup formed by ex-members of Robert What's-his-names's group. Offenbach, for all their laudable endurance as our only balls-to-the-wall blues band and great party animals, will be remembered more for where we were when we listened to the music than for the music itself. Guitar hero Walter Rossi had moments of greatness no one ever heard, whereas Mahogany Rush heard more of its own greatness than it ever created. And April Wine doesn't count, if only because the opportunistic English South Shore band established their power base outside the province by heading off happily in every musical direction at once.

No one can charge Michel "Pag" Pagliaro with the same sins. Pag was Quebec's once and, possibly future, king of rock – from his appearance in the '70s to his active retirement during the '80s and his recent return to the frontlines. He can rave like Little Richard, write pop songs in French and English to make a craftsman weep, and deliver crunching hard rock chords in concert night after night. "Rainshowers", "Some Sing", "Loving You Aint Easy", and " J'Entends Frapper" are classic rock 'n' roll songs that have had Canadian and American critics foaming at the mouth since the early '70s.

Claude Dubois: progressive chansonnier

But through twists of fate and his own undoing, Pagliaro still remains one of Quebec's best kept secrets.

Pag's inability to break the US market wide-open was merely symptomatic of what sent the Quebec music industry into a freefall as the '70s leaned into the '80s. Even as talented solo artists as Diane Tell, Paul Piché, Robert Paquette, Louise Portal, Veronique Beliveau, Daniel Lavoie, and more were shoring up their careers with strong records and tours, the bottom was falling out of album sales in the province.

Blame an international economic recession, the break-up of many of the '70s biggest groups, a provincial spiritual realignment away from nationalism and toward world pop, or the kind of cultural claustrophobia that strikes when too many artists spend too much time together in too small a place; but the fact remains that many pop stars were lucky to sell makers of records the equivalent of their shoe size for most of the '80s.

Thanks to the reversal of some of the above trends, the infusion of new blood, an undeniable improvement in the quality of music created, and other intangibles that make following rock 'n' roll so weird and so much fun, Quebec pop has experienced a recent resurgence no doctor or priest could have predicted.

- Hard-rocking female singer Marjo jettisons and her band Corbeau sells well over 100,000 copies of her debut solo, and tours the province to sold-out shows till she drops;
- Daniel Lavoie pares his music down to electronic grooves and dark vocals, launches two back-to-back albums way over the platinum mark, and becomes a star in France;
- Celine Dion sloughs off her goody-two shoes child-prodigy image, hikes her skirts up to here, and revitalizes her position at 19 as one of the potentially greatest singers in the country;

BLAST

J.B. AND THE PLAYBOYS

BACKGROUND:
This Montreal-based band got its start in the early '60s playing occasional gigs in Quebec. The members were Allan Nicholls, Andy Kaye, Louis Yachnin, Doug West, and Bill Hill. Local critics called them Montreal's Beatles. They later moved to Toronto and changed their name to The Jaybees, and still later to The Carnival Connection.

CLAIMS TO FAME:
In addition to having thousands of teenaged girls from Montreal screaming at their Beatlesque style, the band released such singles as "Chances", "My Delight", "Summer Love", "I'm A Loner", and "Poster Man". They toured eastern Canada and opened for The Rolling Stones.

MUSICAL STYLE:
Pop-rock

WHERE ARE THEY NOW?:
Nicholls went on to star on Broadway in Hair *and* Jesus Christ Superstar. *He had parts in the movies* Nashville, Buffalo Bill and the Indians, *and* Slapshot. *He has worked as an assistant director/screenwriter for Robert Altman, and he directed Leonard Cohen's* I'm A Hotel *music video. He lives in Vermont. Yachnin played for Tommy Graham and the Big Town Boys and Lighthouse, and currently works on drag racing cars at Competitive Automotive in Richmond Hill. Kaye played in Toronto band The Classics, still performs, and also works as a courier for Purolater. Hill owns a recording studio in Montreal, and West was last heard to be working in the computer business in Mississauga.*

QUOTABLE QUOTE:
Nicholls on the band's inability to make it big in the US: "It was frustrating because we had done everything we could do in Canada. The idea of any project was to be received by as many people as possible."

FABULOUS FACT:
The band had orignally been called just The Playboys, but inspired by Playboy magazine, they lengthened the band name because, says Nicholls, "every time you saw an executive or a rich guy in their cartoons, he was called J.B."

· Corey Hart goes after the international gold ring with a vengeance and grabs it first time 'round with "Sunglasses at Night" and million-dollar sales figures. He's slipped now, a result of senseless paranoia, arrogance, and too-much-too-soon. But, all who have been around him lately say that Corey has learned some serious lessons about life and has no intentions of screwing up again;

· The Box win a local talent contest, sign a recording contract, and three albums later are one of the most popular groups in the country. Like Hart, they sing in English, though they're French to a man; unlike him, they've never forgotten who they are;

· Mitsou, the 18-year-old tiny buxom relative of Quebec theatre institution, playwright Gratien Gélinas, picks up a few fashion tips from Madonna, releases a hot teeny-bop single and a hotter teeny-bop album, and becomes this week's star fodder for a grateful gossip press;

· Richard Seguin and Pierre Flynn release solo albums. Both are still touring on the strength of their sales over a year later;

· Gerry Boulet puts out his first solo effort since the demise of Offenbach. No one expects that much from the tungsten-lunged singer; everyone is happily surprised and the public buys 25,000 copies in the first five weeks;

· Veteran singer and resident renaissance man Michel Rivard releases an album called *Un Trou dans les Nuages*. Eighteen months and 150,000 copies later, it is still top on the charts, and Rivard can talk about playing the Amnesty International Concert at Montreal's Olympic Stadium with Bruce Springsteen, Sting, and Peter Gabriel — or about singing harmonies with Crosby, Stills and Nash at the Peace Concert in the Forum;

· Johanne Blouin releases a record called "Merci Felix" that just happens to be on the charts when the great man dies. It goes on to sell over 150,000, and the whole crazy circle is completed.

Maybe those sloppy old patriots were right about Felix after all.

John Griffen is former rock critic and now is movie and entertainment columnist for the Montreal Gazette.

4

ALL OVER THE UNDERGROUND

by Tom Harrison

Although most cultural or political revolutions are born of discontent and strife, Canada's rock 'n' roll uprising was a rebellion against ice hockey. Hockey. Canada's national sport. The sole hinge upon which our national identity – sketchy and anonymous as it sometimes is – hangs. Hockey. Symbol of long, cold, cruel winters. Winter. The reason why so many footloose and liberal-minded Canadians flee to the more temperate climes of British Columbia's West Coast hoping to satisfy the art imperative and foment creative, spiritual, and political unrest.

Winter. Canada has a population of, what, 25 million people? Twenty-three million of us were born in Winnipeg. The other two million live in Toronto and would never admit to having been born in Winnipeg, even if they were.

Winnipeg. Winnipeg once was described by sportswriter and hockey fan, Jim Coleman, as nine months of hard winter followed by three months of bad skating. In Winnipeg, babies have their first pair of blades bronzed. Is it any wonder that one of Canada's celebrated rock stars, Neil Young, is the son of another sports columnist, Scott Young? Is it a coincidence that Neil Young's personal rebellion was not to strap on the Tacks, but a Fender? I, too, was born in Winnipeg, and I know from my teenage years spent as the fourth member of the third line for a Bantam B hockey team, freezing my ass off on the bench, and suffering chilblains, that if you didn't play hockey there was only one other way to survive – to escape – and that was to drop out of the hockey social club and pick up a guitar. What else could a poor boy do? Canada's street-fighting man dropped his gloves in the '60s and willingly took a misconduct. Ejected from the game, he held up a finger to Foster Hewitt and Murray Westgate, the authority and father figures of his youth, and looked elsewhere for inspiration and leadership.

He went underground.

◀ *Neil Young: kind of the iconoclasts*

BLAST

THE UGLY DUCKLINGS

BACKGROUND:
The Ugly Ducklings were a Toronto based band consisting of lead vocalist Dave Bingham, guitarists Glynn Bell and Roger Mayne, bassist John Read, and drummer Robin Boers. All still live in the Toronto area with the exception of Bingham, who lives in Fenelon Falls, Ont. They formed in the 1965 and split in December, 1967.

CLAIMS TO FAME:
Their biggest hit, "Gaslight", hit #1 across Canada. Their first single, "Nothin", won the Battle tle of The New Sounds five times in a row on radio station CHUM in Toronto. Other notable singles include "She Ain't No Use To Me" and "Just In Case You Wonder", the latter highlighted by a blistering lead guitar solo. Their greatest hits album is considered a rarity and some collectors estimate its worth at more than $200.

MUSICAL STYLE:
Garage-style rock

WHERE ARE THEY NOW?
The group has reunited for a number of concerts over the years, but all its members have new careers. Bingham is an auto mechanic in Lindsay, Ont. and has dabbled in several area bands over the years; Read is a manager with a large photographic retail company; Mayne works in video production, editing and broadcasting, and recently moved his business into the old CITY-TV building in Toronto, formerly The Electric Circus, a bar where the band performed during its heyday; Bell operates a commercial art business; and Boers teaches drumming and does session work.

QUOTABLE QUOTE:
Bingham remembers the recording of "Gaslight": "Our record company wanted the band to use other musicians on the record to give us a better chance to get a record deal. We said no. Later, I was lured to New York to do jingle recordings and once in the studio they showed me the song and I couldn't resist."

FABULOUS FACT:
Although "Gaslight" was the Duck's biggest hit, only Bingham was involved in recording the song. It was written by a New York taxi driver and background music was provided by a 17-piece band, including 11 musicians from the Tonight Show.

Underground music in Canada may be unique among similar movements in the rest of the world because so much of it has been a response to winter, that dark arctic shroud that unifies us as a nation and sends so many Canadians into warm coffeehouses, smokey bars, and neon nightclubs to fight out boredom rather than hibernate. In 1967, the world was on the cusp of dramatic changes: student riots in Paris and London; Russian tanks on the Czechoslovakian border; racial violence in Detroit; anti-war marches in Washington; headbashing at the Democratic convention in Chicago; the political assassinations of Martin Luther King and Robert Kennedy. Rock 'n' roll was ahead of these upheavals. It could be said that in 1967 rock 'n' roll anticipated them. A unifying force and a catalyst for social change, rock 'n' roll was smiling beatifically during the summer of love, wailing in protest against the war in Vietnam, discovering itself with the same self-conscious delight with which children discover the differences between boys and girls.

In 1967, Canada, too, was on the cusp of drama, in the form of a state of national emergency. That winter, while most of the country was singing Bobby Gimby's "One little two little three Canadians", better known to us sons and daughters of Confederation as "Canada", theme song to the nation's Centennial celebrations, others were taking their cue from the title of The Ugly Ducklings' album on Yorktown Records: *Somewhere Outside.*

Somewhere Outside was hardly a revolutionary record, but it was a brilliant, 1966-era evocation of The Rolling Stones and Pretty Things. One of its key tracks is a six-minute blues instrumental called "Windy City (Noise At The North End)". Although it may be The Ugly Ducklings' paying tribute to The Stones paying tribute to Chicago's Chess Records (situated at 2120 South Michigan Avenue), it was steeped in atmosphere. It felt like winter. It felt like the suffusion of the warmth and relief one needs to escape from the brutal force of driving snow, to step inside a private conspiratorial world of rhythm-and-blues confidants and rock 'n' roll confederates.

In 1967, while draft dodgers and conscientious objectors were fleeing north, Canadians were debating the question of our identity, battling our supposed inferiority complex, and taking their vacation in Montreal, host of Expo '67. Little did a nation in love with its stylish new leader, Pierre Trudeau, suspect that, beneath the radar of the RCMP, the Canadian underground was poised to surface, brandishing guitars and thermal underwear. Little did it know of the explosive contents of President Charles DeGaulle's "*Québec libre*" speech and how it would rock the foundation of Expo '67 and expose the cracks in our divided dominion. And, of course, little did Canada know of the devastating effects of expansion in the NHL later in the year.

Gordon Lightfoot and fans: *the folk fixture that endures yet*

But some heard and responded to the rumblings of bass guitar and fuzzbox change. Historically, most underground movements have had romantic connotations – the myth that the French Resistance of World War II was comprised of brave and selfless freedom fighters and patriots. Similarly, the birth of the rock underground in the '60s has been coloured rosily and distorted by a backward-looking popular media. Steeped in nostalgia, and besotted with seductive admen and their pitches to the aging baby boomer, the media's tendency is to re-write history. To paraphrase the Strawberry Alarm Clock's exploitation of flower power, contemporary media tends to portray the mid-'60s as "incense and peppermints, the colour of time". If it were, rock 'n' roll's *eminence gris* would be Tommy Sands, and Canada's reigning king would be Bobby Curtola. Instead, rock's underground was a confluence of vital ingredients: Bob Dylan, Jack Kerouac, biker movies, Sky Saxon, Beatle boots, Allen Ginsberg, amphetamines, Herman Hesse, John F. Kennedy, Emma Peel, the draft, Richard Farina, John Lennon, Paul McCartney, The Rolling Stones, LSD, Buddha, Jaguar XKEs, Phil Ochs, The Byrds, the blues, John Coltrane, and marijuana. And more, all of it imbued with its own meaning. The rock 'n' roll underground came from bohemians, beatniks, bluesmen, and The Beatles – a unique synthesis of cultural rebels and pop icons taking their cues from one another. The album of the summer of '67 was *Sergeant Pepper's Lonely Hearts Club Band,* but the song was The Doors' "Light My Fire", and the fuse was lit. For a short time, before it turned in on itself, the underground arose and became, not the counter-culture but, as far as the western world was concerned, the dominant culture.

The Canadian rock underground was different from everything else happening in domestic pop by being a response to world events. As the country, as yet still savouring the promise of its second hundred years, drew closer to the Quebec crisis of 1968, the underground was looking somewhere outside. Inadvertently, the underground was taking Canadian rock into the next decade and anticipating the upheavals to come. The stirrings underground weren't necessarily visionary or unified but rather innocent and distinctly regional. Returning to Winnipeg for a minute, I remember hearing those distant rumblings in the unlikely performance, on a TV talent contest no less, of a song called "Psychedelia". I sing it still – the dumbest train wreck of naiveté and epiphany I've ever known. I would have scoffed and sneered and gone back to singing "Hang On, Sloopy" had it not been written and sung by Colin Sexsmith, older brother of a schoolmate. He became an overnight guru of flower power and psychedelic music in the suburb of Westwood. A few months later, some of his classmates were back on TV, this time because marijuana had been found in their high-school locker. The world opened up and closed in at the same time.

Suddenly, I'm singing "The Ballad of a Thin Man" and darkly intoning. "There's something happening here, but you don't know what it is, do you, Mr. Jones?" Suddenly I'm losing interest in being the fourth man on the third line of my Bantam B hockey team.

What separated Colin Sexsmith and his friends from the rest of us was that they were looking outward, bringing home what they saw, giving birth to personal expression and style. Colin had identified a different way of viewing the world, and that revelation immediately changed him as well.

In other words, if Canadian culture tended to be provincial or parochial, the nascent

BLAST

THE PAUPERS

BACKGROUND:
The Paupers, formed in Toronto in the mid-'60s, became one of the first Canadian bands to succeed in the US. Members were Skip Prokop, Chuck Beal, Denny Gerrard, and Bill Marion, who was later replaced by Adam Mitchell.

CLAIMS TO FAME:
The band released two albums, Magic People *and* Ellis Island, *and had success with the singles "Simple Deed" and "If I Call You by Some Name". They also gained prominence in the US when they played on the same bill as The Jefferson Airplane at the Cafe A Go Go in New York. Although they were the opening act, the critics raved about their performance and all but ignored The Jefferson Airplane. The Paupers then signed with influential agent Albert Grossman and toured the US.*

MUSICAL STYLE:
In Prokop's words, "heavy duty, folk-rock psychedelic"

WHERE ARE THEY NOW?:
Prokop left The Paupers to form Lighthouse. He later worked at radio station CFNY, and is now with an advertising firm. Beal worked as a music producer and manager, and now works at the Canadian National Institute for the Blind producing the talking book series. Gerrard played with groups such as Jericho and Luke and the Apostles, and, until 1988 worked at Tippet Richardson. Marion is a successful jingle and commercials singer. Mitchell performed solo in the 1970s and is now a screenwriter in Los Angeles.

QUOTABLE QUOTE:
Beal on why few Canadian bands up to that time succeeded south of the border: "There certainly is a Canadian attitude that you practise until you're perfect and then you take a step. Whereas the American attitude is just to go for it. There were a lot of bands in Canada that probably could have gone down there; but for one reason or another had an attitude that they weren't good enough or they weren't ready."

FABULOUS FACT:
"If I Call You By Some Name", a slow ballad, was the group's biggest hit; but members don't speak of it fondly. Beal says it was "hokey", and Prokop dismisses it as not being "in any way, shape, or form representative of what The Paupers were." The song cracked the Canadian Top 10.

Joni Mitchell: Yorkville's sleeping beauty

underground was making some of us worldly. That worldliness had an effect.

In the late '80s, Yorkville is over-priced bistros and chi-chi boutiques, many loops higher in the spiral of upward mobility than when it arrived on the TV news in the late '60s as Canada's Greenwich Village. It was there on a Toronto street running perpendicular to Yonge and Bay streets and Avenue Road that Canada's one true claim to a musical identity began to take shape, thanks to such clubs as Bernie Fiedler's The Riverboat, The Mousehole, Avenue Club or Purple Onion, home to Bruce Cockburn, Murray McLauchlan, and Dan Hill, as well as to

The Mandala: Toronto's infatuation with R & B

Carole Pope: purveyor of shock and style

Gordon Lightfoot, Ian and Sylvia, and Joni Mitchell before them.

These artists, and many more, married their Canadian heritage to folk, country, blues, and a smattering of rock 'n' roll. They took over the spotlight from the rockabilly being produced by Rompin' Ronnie Hawkins and his ever-changing lazy Susan of rock 'n' roll bands, The Hawks. If Hawkins had put Yonge Street on the map in 1959 by goosing staid ol' Toronto – the city that fun forgot – with a pinch of Mary Lou and a squeeze of Dizzy Miss Lizzie, it was Neil Young, Buffy Ste. Marie, and Lightfoot who tweaked the country's self-awareness with songs of old laughing ladies, go-go girls, and universal soldiers. If Uncle Ronnie brought a reckless rockabilly fever to Yonge Street's Coq D'Or Tavern – where Levon and The Hawks were establishing themselves as the coolest band on the big empty face of the nation – and his Hawk's Nest, Fiedler was introducing Muddy Waters to Canada and providing Canadian songwriters with a springboard to New York.

Until Ronnie Hawkins shook down the city with a Bo Diddley beat and played midwife to Downchild, Whiskey Howl, and Crowbar, Yonge Street in the late '50s and early '60s was The First Floor of the Colonial, legendary jazz clubs where you could see a great such as Earl Hines for a two-beer minimum. It was The Bluenote, where rhythm and blues was the elicit truth, the bump and grinding facts of life, the womb to The Mandala and David Clayton Thomas.

And then the folk revival happened in New York and Boston and Toronto – in Yorkville where, as early as 1961, folk was Canada's true underground. As Yorkville's identity took shape, it transformed itself into a repository of thought, ideas, youthful rebellion, and, inevitably, rock 'n' roll. By this time, in 1967, Levon and The Hawks already had signed their pact with Bob Dylan. Taking their place

Skinny Puppy: sturm und drang from Gastown, B.C. ▶

were The Paupers, Kensington Market, Rick James and Neil Young's Mynah Birds, and John Kay's Sparrow. David Clayton Thomas was singing his amazing jazz-protest garage-rock anthem, "Brainwashed", and those Ugly Ducklings were putting out records on the Yorkville label.

Rock 'n' roll moved in and squatted on folkie turf, bringing with it an embryonic counter-culture interested in loud music, sex, protest, and driven by a sense of purpose. There was no gap between the audience and the performers; they were joined by their common bonds and ideals. The clubs and the bars existed for them, and a label such as Yorkville did its best to ride its brief momentum. At its height, which coincided with the bloom of the hippy and the glare of the national media, Yorkville was producing the country's most enduring, influential, uniquely Canadian rock and pop music. It started as a low-rent enclave governed by artists, peaked in 1966-67, and ended by being bought out by developers who had hosed it down and spiffed it up by 1970.

Alas, this seems to be true of most music that has come out of Toronto since then. By 1970, Canadian content regulations were in place and Toronto was the acknowledged centre of the music business. Many of those who had come to Yorkville for its reckless disregard for convention soon were surprised to discover that, by the '80s, they were The Establishment.

Over the years, the occasional pimple of unrest and opposition has burst and left its scar behind. There were big scenes on Spadina at the El Mocambo, punk rock and Nazi Dog's Viletones, Rough Trade's shock value, and, on Queen Street, Parachute Club's evocation of World Beat — entirely in keeping with Toronto's acquired cosmopolitan metabolism. Mostly, the city's identity as a centre of commerce likewise has influenced all but those vestiges of Yorkville's influence: The Cameron House, Rivoli, Bamboo or Horseshoe.

Odd as it may seem, the story of Montreal's underground has had a similar conclusion. Once upon a time, while the Montreal Canadiens were stocking up on Stanley Cup rings and being downright arrogant about it, howls of protest were heard above the noise of the city's east end, and being felt all the way to its west end. The Quebeçois, tired of being treated like the white niggers of North America, were finding their voice in two modes of expression — political activism and music.

Both were there to be heard in the early '60s in conversations at the jazz clubs such as the Black Bottom, where Oscar Peterson and his musical siblings were the royal family to whose court such influential jazz players as Michael Donato and Oliver Lake gravitated. The Black Bottom was the hottest jazz club in the city, and existed in a cabaret environment of Crescent Street bars, booze, broads, blues, blacks, and blackjack.

Like the province, Montreal was divided

Chalk Circle: Toronto's brave new generation

Leroy Sibbles: black Toronto's cross-over reggae success

by the haves of the West and have nots of the East, by English and French cultures, by the West's thriving live music and the East's do-it-yourself idealism. Music held both halves together. In the '60s and early '70s, Crescent Street's bars and cafes, such as the Yellow Door and Crêpe Bretonne, were both focal points and community listening posts for the foment of art and music that identified the nascent underground.

You could hang out on Crescent Street, buy a sound system, jive with the blacks, maybe score some dope, but you had to be cleared. You had to know somebody who could give you a clean bill of health. Crescent Street had to know that you weren't either a narc or that your political activities weren't being monitored by the RCMP.

Today, a broadcaster with CBUF Radio in Vancouver and a concert promoter, André Rheaume remembers that when he was playing guitar with the Ville Emard Blues Band, it was the expression that was more important to the musicians than the finished product. "The East side didn't have money, but the music it made was a co-operative effort. The Ville Emard Blues Band formed the nucleus of a scene in the community of Ville Emard around which such stars as Charles DeBois and Robert Charlebois would gather when they needed a band or to record in the band's own studio. We bridged the division between the English and French scenes."

The Ville Emard Blues Band was a huge, sprawling co-operative of musicians, artists, writers, and creative people who couldn't bring their many tangents of energy and drive under control. It was, however, a reservoir of thought and action that only could have existed in the late '60s. Rock 'n' roll was alive in Montreal where The Haunted, Michel Pagliaro, J.B. And The Playboys, and The Rabble were talking to fans in both languages. There was disquiet, however, and a simmering Quebec nationalism that gibed with the hippie idealism of the mid-'60s, and was stimulated by the province's stringent Catholicism.

If the church reinforced the Quebeçois identity and aggravated its alienation from English-speaking Canada in the summer of 1967, Charles De Gaulle visited Expo, uttered his historic "*Québec libre*" speech, and the *bonhomie* of the Centennial was wiped away forever. André Rheaume compared the speech to a bomb going off. The shock waves were felt as far away as Vancouver and, with the explosion of the Quebec Crisis and Trudeau's declaration of martial law the following year, the province's musicians and artists were sucked into the turmoil, try as they might to separate themselves from the extremism of the FLQ.

By that time, Rheaume was a broadcaster for one of Canada's first FM rock stations, CHOM, having graduated from LS Radio, a free-form experiment that, among other adventures, gave equal time to the FLQ and musicians alike. This Montreal was radically removed from the McGill University scene and its most famous pop artists — Paul Anka, Leonard Cohen or Galt McDermot (co-writer of the hippie musical, *Hair*). One song that embraced and encapsulated French-Canadian anger and pride was "Lindberg!!!". Sung by Robert Charlebois and taken from the satirical, barbed musical *Osti d' Show*, it crystalized the religious and political forces exerting their influence on the province, and set the tone for the next decade. Out of this underground-fostered Quebeçois pride came a phenomenally prosperous and fruitful period in French-Canadian music, which created superstars of Harmonium, Ginette Reno, Michel Pagliaro, Michel Rivard, and Beau Dommage.

However, as separatism lost its impetus and its jockeys, the Partie Quebeçois, fell from grace, so too did Quebec's music. Today, there is money in Quebec and a conservatism has taken the reins. As André Rheaume sees it, the beginning of the end came when CHOM attempted to air a live broadcast of the massed might of the Ville Emard Blues Band — 75 musicians strong playing for all they were worth from the collective's own studio warehouse. It caught fire and burned down while they all went out for sandwiches. Nobody knows how or why it could have happened.

Now, 15 years later, Quebec has Musique Plus, heavy metal, Og! Records, and the Cargo label. Dance music and Euro-pop are forming the consciousness of the province's youth, and little produced there bears the stamp of a local culture.

If conflict gave bored, disaffected youth and beatnik intellectuals a weapon with which to combat the bitter winds of winter in the East, it has been a motivational tool on the temperate West Coast, the eye of which was (and is) Vancouver. If an underground movement to parallel the activism of the '60s still exists in Canada, it is here in the city usually characterized east of Chilliwack as "Lotusland".

B.C. seems destined to be a province of extremes, and Vancouver always will be its apotheosis. Sleeping on park benches amid nature's unparalleled splendour are a legion of bag men and bag ladies. Although its waterfront is laden with wheat from Alberta and cars from Korea, the city's food banks are criminally barren.

The paradox hasn't gone unnoticed by the city's creative segment, a substantial part of which was attracted to Vancouver by its artistic environment and, of course, its milder temperatures. Walking the streets of Gastown, the oldest section of Vancouver, it is possible still to feel the pulse of radical or alternative culture embodied in its art, music, and politics, which in large part are byproducts of transience and restlessness.

Gastown is where students from the Emily Carr School of Art and punks from the suburbs collided and merged in a youth's uprising in 1977. More than 10 years later, the impact is still felt. It isn't necessary to be heard in the rock clubs, as there are fewer of them now than a few years ago, or seen in the favoured cafes or galleries, as they are spread from Commercial Street (Joe's Cafe is a popular boho hang out) to Kitsilano (a neighbourhood of the University of B.C.). But it still is there in heart and mind, and a closer look at Vancouver's "alternative" community reveals its parallels with, and a deep lineage to, the city's happy hippie days of the late '60s.

Back then, The Seeds Of Time were rocking out the anthemic "My Hometown" and The Collectors were singing "17th Summer", a tribal song that did the strange trick of evoking the spirit of West Coast Indian heritage, of recalling 17 years of rock-and-roll, and telling the story of a pregnant girl and woman-to-be. They would sing it at Love-Ins and Be-Ins at Stanley Park, where the new tribes gathered at Easter to dance and to tell themselves that a peaceful revolution was at hand.

On the streets of Gastown, and particularly on Fourth Avenue in Kitsilano, were hundreds of girls whose story was similar to that of "17th Summer". While their boyfriends might be out on the street, trying to score dope or coffee, tourists could spot them hanging out at Cool Aid, reading *The Georgia Straight*, voice of the underground.

In 1968, Vancouver was home to transients who'd hitchhiked from as far away as Montreal and draft resistors from the US who'd fled the country's military madness. They all were here to crash on the beaches and soak up the vibes. This, indeed, was the new Mother Nature taking over.

Or would have been, were it not for the reactionary forces of Mayor Tom Campbell. Campbell was scandalized by the free-loving, free-living, freeloading hippies, and ranted long and loud about how they were the reason for society's moral decay and were ruining Vancouver's tourist appeal. If he'd had any vision, Campbell would have seen that the hippies had become a tourist attraction in themselves. The Summer of Love had arrived the previous year, the underground had endorsed it, and it had blossomed (as flower power was wont to do). Overnight, Vancouver was Canada's San Francisco; Fourth Avenue was its Haight Ashbury. An immigrant artist, Joachim Foikus, was given a Canada Council Grant to serve as a harlequinlike Town Fool. Mr. Peanut, a perform-

Molly Johnson and Alta Moda: darlings of the Queen Street set

ance artist, would attend counter-culture events and give the festivities his blessing. "Harold Head", a weekly comic strip drawn by Rand Holmes that ran in the pages of the *Straight*, gave the community a cartoon hero who expressed the ideals of the hippie culture and satirized the rabid, redneck foaming at the mouth of Campbell.

Without knowing it, Tom Campbell gave the local underground its own Vietnam to fight. His efforts to shut down Cool Aid (a neighbourhood halfway house for runaways and kids coming down off bad drug trips), to ban the Be-Ins at Stanley Park, to sweep the hippies off the beach, to infiltrate such rock clubs as the Retinal Circus and Afterthought, and to bust *The Georgia Straight* only succeeded in distilling the war of ideologies into an Us vs. Them conflict — hip versus straight society; youth culture versus The Establishment.

The tension mounted and festered until, in 1970, a rally to campaign for the legalization of marijuana was organized in Gastown outside the front door of *The Georgia Straight*. The Smoke-In started as a peaceful demonstration but ended as a bloody riot when Vancouver police charged into the crowd on foot and horseback to disperse the demonstrators and arrest those who'd dared to light up in public. It was a disgraceful night in the confrontation between Campbell and the underground. In the aftermath, Campbell's political spirit was broken and he did not bother to seek another term of office. Yet his work was complete.

That summer, Vancouver's Seeds of Time returned from a brief sojourn in Eastern Canada, where the band had lived in Montreal, convinced that it accidentally had rented a house shared by FLQ terrorists and under surveillance by the RCMP. The experience did no good for their drug-induced paranoia, and they'd come back to Vancouver to find that the underground that had made them outlaw heroes in 1968 was fleeing for the hippie communes on Vancouver Island and up the West Coast.

What was happening in Vancouver was happening wherever a seething, vibrant arts community had had its energy sapped by too many conflicts and drugs, half-baked ideology, and misguided philosophy, inner turmoil, and opportunism.

Captain Beefheart has a theory that the American underground was destroyed by *Rolling Stone* Magazine. He believes that as the counter-culture was on the rise, each community had its own voice in the form of underground publications such as the *L.A. Free Press*. The movement was unified and linked by regional newspapers that addressed the particular issues and concerns of their community. As long as these thrived, record companies and other youth marketeers who, in turn, thrived by exploiting the new age of

54 40: psychedelic retrofit from the West Coast

rock while never understanding it, had to advertise in them all, thereby supporting and cultivating the movement.

As *Rolling Stone* became identified nationwide as the authoritive voice of rock and the underground, the recording industry and national advertisers could reach the market by concentrating advertising budgets on one magazine (and a few likely contenders). *Rolling Stone*'s rise was the underground press's fall. By the mid-'70s, most of the radical alternative weeklies were gone and the hippies slipped into the warm bath of the '70s to meet life's challenges all sensible and self-satisfied as the yuppies of the '80s.

Most of them, anyway. Vancouver's hippie consciousness abated but never died; it dispersed but it didn't surrender altogether.

Through the '70s, *The Georgia Straight* found ways to survive. *The Straight* was never courted by national advertisers, but spent time in a lot of courts anyway. When the punks invaded Vancouver from the satellites and suburbs of Surrey and Burnaby and White Rock, led by such politically-motivated types as Joey Shithead of DOA and rock 'n' roll dangerboys as Art Bergmann, *The Straight* got on the new wave, regained its street smarts, shed its hippie image and, by 1988, developed into a non-threatening but comprehensive weekly lifestyle magazine. From the dilapidated building on Powell Street in Gastown to the chilly upstairs office in Kitsilano next door to Greenpeace, to its corporate-looking digs near the business section of Vancouver's West End, Dan McLeod's *Georgia Straight* has been a mirror of the rise and fall and shifting of the West Coast's rock underground.

Whereas the fate of Vancouver's rock underground was similar to movements in the rest of the country in that it relied on a base of support from within and information from without – either in the form of print, FM rock radio or visiting rock bands – its insu-

Erroll Starr and Billy Newton-Davis: new soul mates

lar existence on the West Coast means that it held no longer than most.

The city's attractiveness to artists and activists alike, its distance from the centre of the Canadian music industry and close proximity to San Francisco and L.A., historically have meant that its rock music has been political in thought and action whereas its musicians have staunchly guarded the integrity of their work from conception to completed artwork.

In the '80s, the punks and art students took over from the hippies, rejecting their Aquarian bean sprout nonsense and nonviolence, at least at first. They did, however, take a page out of hippie history in staging a Be-In style gathering in 1978 in Stanley Park called Anarchy in the Park. It was there that punks and anarchists met under the influence of The Sex Pistols, and the character of West Coast punk began to take shape.

The day was headlined by DOA, which, despite battles with white power Nazis in San Francisco and onstage fights at home, has soldiered on for more than a decade, ideals intact. Whatever the issue, DOA has been there, lending its support and growing brute strength. In 1982, when the Squamish Five, a collection of Vancouver anarchists, Groucho Marxists, and punks, went on trial for allegedly fire-bombing video stores, a B.C. Hydro power station, and a Litton Industries factory in Ontario, DOA recorded a single to help raise money for court costs and to demonstrate its loyalty to the group's friend, Gerry Hannah, former bassist for The Subhumans – another band that had appeared at Anarchy in the Park. A year later, when the province's unions were on the eve of a general strike to show their disapproval of the Socred government's labour bashing, DOA likewise recorded General Strike as an act of solidarity.

And so it has gone on. At its best, Van-

Tom Cochrane: an earnest and angry guitar hero

couver rock 'n' roll has always acted with good conscience and faith. It has responded to issues in the community and on the road.

In 40 years of rock, Vancouver has had its share of scenes: Les Vogt and Red Robinson's rock 'n' roll shows in the '50s, its coffee-house folk circle, its mid-'60s R&B show-bands, its late '60s acid-rock, '70s punk assault, and '80s alternative record industry led by the internationalist Nettwerk label. But they've all arisen out of a spirit of independence and proceeded with a willful individuality. To outsiders, this spirit is quaintly out of step with the times, if not outright anachronistic; but it has kept rock 'n' roll alive on the West Coast. Knowing that has kept at least a few musicians warm and dry during the winter months — and probably ruined a few promising careers in hockey!

Tom Harrison is rock critic for the Vancouver Province and leader of his own band, Bruno Gerussi's Medallion.

5
THE BOYS IN THE BANDS

by Lorraine Segato

Chilliwack: Light-headed pop from the West Coast

hen I was asked to write a chapter on "men" in the Canadian music business, my first reaction was, "Are you kidding? I mean, given my reputation as a big bad feminist, why are they asking me?"

But soon I found myself wandering through archives in the library, talking to everyone who seems to remember and, admittedly, becoming obsessed with finding out what I could about men in music. And despite my initial reaction, I've come to feel a kind of kinship, a concern about the impact that these artists may or may not have had on the development of music in this country over the past 30-odd years. It also seemed like an opportunity to evalulate my own contradictory feelings about the business of music. I decided to start just around the time of the emergence of rock and roll, the magic year 1952, four years before I emerged from my mommy's tummy.

The politics and climate of the '50s was extremely conservative and anti-sex; McCarthyite commie-bashing was popular and the basic *Leave It To Beaver* family structure was the given. Yet, from the fringes of the entertainment scene arose the fascination of TV and the taboo delights of Elvis' and Jerry Lee Lewis' rock 'n' roll. The combination sparked the hearts of teenagers, and terrified the minds of parents everywhere.

Although very little Canadian-produced or recorded music in the early '50s was original, a turn of the dial in 1952 would have brought you a song called "The Little White Cloud That Cried" performed by an emotional singer by the name of Johnny Ray. The mid-'50s also saw the arrival of a vocal act called the Four Lads who, coincidentally or perhaps not so coincidentally, had been the arrangers for the backgrounds on Johnny Ray's second single "Cry". Although the Four Lads began their recording career in 1952 with a song called "Mockingbird", it wasn't until 1955 that they had a big hit: "Moments to Remember". From this hit, they went on

Corey Hart: the lout with the pout ▶

to record many top ten singles until the original group disbanded in the late 1950s.

Another group to surface at about this time was a Toronto vocal group called the Canadaires (sounds like an airline, doesn't it?), who later became known as the Crew-cuts. It took them some time to find their name, let alone fame and fortune, and, like most musicians, they followed all the avenues toward their "big break". While still the Canadaires, they drove to New York in 1952 to appear on the influential program *Arthur Godfrey' Talent Hunt*; although they won second place, their "big" win got them work in little else but seedy nightclubs in the eastern States and Canada. Months later, on a below-zero day in Sudbury, a call came through informing them that a guest spot on the *Gene Carroll Show* waited at the end of a 600-mile drive south to Cleveland. They did it, and after the show they were introduced to local DJ Billy Randle who suggested that they call themselves The Crew-cuts because of their hairstyle. He also introduced them to Mercury Records. In 1954, they came out with their first hit "Crazy 'Bout You". They had a follow-up song in 1954 that became the No.1 record in North America: "Sh-Boom".

The next vocal group to make itself known was a group called The Diamonds. Signed to Mercury Records by Billy Randle, the same DJ who supported The Crewcuts, they – like many of the vocal groups at the time – became successful by appropriating black R&B tunes. In fact, their inspiration came from an unknown black group from Detroit named The Revelaires. I was only two or three at the time, but I remember the hits such as "Little Darlin" and "Why Do Fools Fall in Love" by the Diamonds rather vividly.

It was through exposure on TV that most artists in the '50s became widely known. Other than travelling around Canada in search of new places that would let them play for, at most, beer money, the approach then seemed fairly clear: get on TV, have someone hear you, and get yourself a deal.

These musicians didn't have the integrated multi-media machine that exists today to promote them and their records. Although television played an extraordinary large role in a '50s group's quest for fame, there were promotional tours that would consist of appearances at record stores or the opening of retail stores in local suburbs – or an appearance at a school sockhop – that would inevitably get the music heard. Walt Grealis, publisher of *RPM Magazine* remembers: "Back in the old days of radio, you could walk into CHUM with a record, and go up to Bob Macadorey or Al Slaight and say, 'Hey, I really believe in this record', and they would play it right there. I was amazed because the switchboard would light up. That was how some hits were made."

As we moved into the 1960s, the Kennedy years would influence a slow opening of liberal sentiment, and the entry of the US into the Vietnam war would blast the lid off Pandora's proverbial box. With the blooming of flower power and the back-to-the-land hippie idealism, we found ourselves in this country profoundly affected by our neighbours.

BLAST

A FOOT IN COLDWATER

BACKGROUND:
A Foot in Coldwater began on a farm in Brougham, Ont., developing out of the Toronto bands Nucleus and Island. Some of the members had also been in the popular Toronto teen band, The Lords of London. Members of A Foot In Coldwater were Paul Naumann, Danny Taylor, Alex Machin, Hughie Leggat, and Bob Horne. Toronto was their home base, but they played concerts throughout Canada.

CLAIMS TO FAME:
During its seven years, the band recorded a number of albums and singles including its biggest hit the rock classic "Make Me Do Anything You Want", which climbed high on charts in 1972 and 1974. Their other singles included "In My Life" and "Love Is Coming", and the band once played before 100,000 at a rock concert in Vermont.

MUSICAL STYLE:
Heavy rock

WHERE ARE THE NOW?"
After the group disbanded in 1977, Leggat took a break from the business and then later went solo, releasing an album Illuminations *in 1981. He is still writing songs (one recently cut by Blue Oyster Cult), and has worked driving a tractor trailer. He now lives in Toronto. Machin did some songwriting in Los Angeles and had some solo singing projects. He had some bad luck with record companies, but stayed in the business. He sings on commercials for companies such as Chrysler, Hostess, and Molson and in 1988 was preparing an album. He, too, lives in Toronto. Taylor, too, does session work, but also owns a furniture and carpet-cleaning business. He lives in Pickering. Naumann, who has lived in Texas and Toronto, still plays and produces music,. Horne, who lives in Las Vegas, has a pool cleaning business. The band reunited in 1988 for a series of summer concerts throughout Ontario. They took a break from the road in the fall and concentrated on songwriting. They are considering doing a new album.*

QUOTABLE QUOTE:
"'Make Me Do Anything You Want.' There was a freshness to it. But that song wasn't even very representative of the way the band sounded. We were a much heavier band than that song."

FABULOUS FACT:
The band's name is one of the stranger ones in Canadian rock music history. The name A Foot in Coldwater is taken from a saying that means the situation a person is in when he or she has made a wrong turn. More realistically, it refers to someone who's in deep shit.

Yet, for a long time, there was little discernable effect on the music. Instead, two things sum up the image of the most famous performer to dominate the late '50s and early '60s music scene: gold chains and a seamless tan line, and the one and only Paul Anka, a self-declared rebel of a teenager. Our new teenage idol was from Ottawa. He has said he was a bad boy when he was in school. If you use distraction as a meter of "badness", then we've all been bad. A teenager with a healthy self-interest, he'd ask vocal groups playing in Parliament town to his father's restaurant after the show. Finally, his father, no longer able to restrain his son from pursuing his dream of stardom, lent him the money to travel to New York so he could visit the record companies and music publisher's offices. It so happened that he stayed with another popular vocal group out of Canada: The Rover Boys. I saw some film footage of his stay there, and I got this image of a little boy being teased by these young men. He didn't seem to mind though; it looked as though he was having the time of his life. He probably knew what the others didn't – that no matter what, he was gonna land himself a deal. And he did. With an introduction to the same producer that signed the Rover Boys, Anka was impressive enough to get himself a contract with ABC/Paramount. Mr. Costa didn't have to worry, for Paul delivered a smash hit with his first single "Diana". 1957: I was only a year old, and this enthusiastic teenager was travelling around the States and Europe singing his heart out. He took his job as a teen idol very seriously; he would often take to comforting and counselling his adoring constituency by writing back, with brief Ann Landers type advice. One letter reads: "Should I kiss a boy on my first date?" His cautious wisdom replies: "Keep calm and all will go well." With a fan club membership of over 60,000 in Canada alone, I hope no one took the advice too seriously. Anyway, the guy is now a millionaire living in the U.S. The lesson in all this? Have chutzpah, will travel.

The next teen idol to hit our stage was Thunder Bay boy, Bobby Curtola. His first single, "Hand in Hand", recorded in 1960, wasn't an immediate hit. For Curtola – as for Anka – persistence was the key to success. Eventually, the song went to number one in Winnipeg, and that was the beginning of many TV appearances that augmented his school studies. His appeal was due largely to his clean-cut looks, I suppose – quite the opposite in image to, say, a Gino Vanelli. Most men I've talked to did not particularly relate to Bobby. They found his gold lamé suits lame. TV clips of him show that he tended to move from side to side a lot, rather than the hip swivelling libido rolls that made Elvis spark; Bobby was more like Frankie Avalon, where the action was mostly in the rolling eyes and dimples.

Again, appearances probably had a lot to do with his popularity. Bobby was the first Canadian to capitalize on this new medium by understanding that movement was a key element in television image-making. The introduction of TV certainly began to affect the way performers began to present themselves.

Yet, an uninterrupted hour with Bobby Curtola and I'm still confused about his mass appeal. Like Paul Anka, young Bobby was exciting the nubile hearts of teen gals across the country. I don't get it. I know looks are a relative thing and fame a matter of time and place, but as I shuffle through the information, it becomes clear that men don't have to look good to be either popular or fashionable. I mean they might be intense, smart, effeminate or rough-and-tumble – even drunks – but unlike their women counterparts, they weren't judged primarily by their looks.

BLAST

LEIGH ASHFORD

BACKGROUND:
The Toronto rock group Leigh Ashford formed in 1966 as members were finishing high school. The group lasted until 1971, gaining a wide following throughout Canada and parts of the US along the way. Among the members over the years were Gord Waszek (guitar), Wally Cameron (drums), Buzz Sherman (vocals), Joe Agnello (bass), Newton Garwood (keyboards), and Don Elliot (bass). They broke up because of creative difference and management problems.

CLAIMS TO FAME:
The band had a solid following in Toronto music circles. They were known for their trademark opening of concerts by playing the theme for 2001 – A Space Odyssey. *Leigh Ashford recorded two albums, the second,* Kinfolk, *being the most successful. Their most widely known single was "Dickens". They recorded in New York City, opened for The Who at The Rockpile, performed with Vanilla Fudge, and played the Strawberry Fields Festival in Mosport, Ont. before an estimated 150,000 music fans.*

MUSICAL STYLE:
Rock

WHERE ARE THEY NOW?:
Waszek played in a number of bands after Leigh Ashford, including Fludd and Burgundy. He lives in Unionville, Ont., continues to write, and plays in Toronto, most notably with singer Bobby Dupont, formerly of Sweet Blindness. As for some of the other members, Waszek says Cameron is also still playing in Toronto; Garwood was store manager at Long and McQuade music store in Toronto; Elliot is an audio technician and cameraman. Shearman, who later attained fame with rock group Moxy, was killed in a motorcycle accident.

QUOTABLE QUOTE:
Waszek on the benefits of the CRTC ruling that made radio stations play a certain amount of Canadian music: "I was glad to see the rules change because we and a lot of other bands weren't being recognized by radio stations. I think we were overall better players than our counterparts in the US."

FABULOUS FACT:
When Waszek was at Riverdale Collegiate, he gave guitar lessons to a younger kid named Hughie Leggat. That young kid went on to play with The Lords of London, and then gain Canada-wide fame as a member of A Foot In Coldwater.

Perhaps the most prevailing music to affect us over the years, and the music we were most recognized for outside this country initially, was folk music. As early as 1961, musicians such as Gordon Lightfoot and Ian and Sylvia were strumming the chords of change. The initial recognition accorded Lightfoot's "Lovin' Me" and "Early Morning Rain", as well as their own songs, unleashed a wave of popularity for singer-songwriters within the next decade. Their offspring included Murray McLauchlan, Bruce Cockburn, Leonard Cohen, and Neil Young.

Ian Tyson, a lover of country music and rodeos, came to music by way of an accident that landed him in the hospital; his aunt brought a guitar to pass some time. A fellow hospital roommate knew some chords and from there he started his apprenticeship with the muse of music. Time passed; he studied art, frequented the local Vancouver coffee house scene, and began singing in a house band for $40 a week at the New Delhi Chop Suey Parlor. Later he'd made his way to Toronto where he met Sylvia Fricker; they later became a duo both professionally and personally. It is said that it was in fact Sylvia who brought the folk influence to the music while Ian himself was more influenced by rockabilly. Soon, restless from the circuit in Toronto, they headed to New York where they met Albert Grossman, who was also manager to Bob Dylan and Peter, Paul and Mary. Later, through Ian and Sylvia's introduction, Grossman signed both Gordon Lightfoot and Murray McLauchlan.

Tyson and Lightfoot have many differences, to be sure, but they were the most influential artists of the '60s and '70s that truly spoke of a sense of Canadian place. Their poetic introspection and prairie-painted imagery, always remind me of driving across this country on the Trans-Canada Highway on to the next gig. Tyson's classic "Four Strong Winds" always comes to mind when I think of the vast magnificence of this country's landscape. Both Tyson and Lightfoot had international as well as domestic recognition in their early recording career. Lightfoot himself has been called the definitive Canadian singer-songwriter. He is a man who has walked the path of both poetic inspiration and personal pathos, creating an awesome repertoire of memorable songs while struggling with personal crises, privately and publicly. Whatever I may think of the dominant duality between romance and the contempt that he appears to feel about

Frank Marino and Mahogany Rush: the big guitar sound ▶

the women in his life, I also balance that with the fact that it takes a strong individual to take his life back into his own hands by accepting the challenge of a life without alcohol.

The Guess Who originally hit the air waves in 1964 with a single called "Shakin' All Over", which was big for them both in Canada and the US. Burton Cummings was not in the group then. A fellow named Chad Allen was. When Chad left the band, Randy Bachman hired Cummings, who was described as being "a wild punk singer who would destroy pianos by jumping on them with high-heeled boots."

With songs, such as "Laughin'/Undone" and, much later, "American Woman", The Guess Who remains one of Canada's most recognizable groups. There has been much said about the internal conflict within the band toward the end. I do admit to being offended hearing Burton Cummings go on about how he hated women. But, hey, we all have our bad days. I just wish that I could get away with having them in public as he did.

Toward the late '60s and early '70s, various musical strains infected Canada. The end of the folk-bohemian coffee-house era spilled into the hippy movement and anti-Vietnam war sentiment, and music spanned from folk to country rock. We found ourselves blessed with the possibility of listening to the R&B sounds of David Clayton Thomas and The Shays, Mandala, and Shawne Jackson. Vancouver's music scene was likewise diverse. With the arrival of American draft dodgers, who came up avoiding the war, the street corners were filled with musicians busking for a dollar. In the local Gastown bars – an area much like Toronto's Yorkville – you could hear any number of bands. At that time, clubs such as Big Mother, the Retinal Gallery, and the Afterthought would showcase bands with equally incongruous names such as Papa Bear's Medicine Show, Hydro Electric Streetcar or Mother Tucker's Yellow Duck on a nightly basis. It was, however, The Collectors (later known as Chilliwack) and the Tom Northcott Trio who had the strongest foothold in the music scene of the west at the time.

TV, too, became more sophisticated in its coverage of Canadian music, although shows such as *Stompin' Tom Connors* and *Country Hoedown* dominated the Canadian-produced TV weekly series. There were American imports – such as Ronnie Hawkins. A veteran of several record contracts, he's had his share of ups and downs. In the late '60s, he was best known for his gigs at Toronto's L'Coq d'Or where he performed with The Hawks. Ronnie has perhaps had more people go through his bands than anyone else in this country. A relentless rehearsal maniac, he would even practise after a show. Many great musicians have cut their teeth in Ronnie's band, rock 'n' roll soldiers every last one of them.

All across the country there seemed to be pockets of musical diversity thriving, from

BLAST

GODDO

BACKGROUND:
Goddo, the "pretty bad boys" of Canadian rock, formed in the mid-'70s. Original members were leader, songwriter, bass player, and former member of Fludd, Greg Godovitz, guitarist Gino Scarpelli, and drummer Marty Morin. Morin left the band early and was replaced by Doug Inglis. The band played together for about 10 years and broke up in the mid-'80s. They reunited in early 1989 for a series of concerts and club gigs.

CLAIMS TO FAME:
Goddo was best known for its powerhouse live show, its wild stage-antics, and a reputation as a group that liked to party long after the performing was done. They played throughout Canada, and had some of their greatest successes in hometown Toronto, where they performed at Maple Leaf Gardens and various concert halls and clubs. They also had a strong following in Vancouver and Winnipeg. The band's most successful single was "Pretty Bad Boy". They also released several albums including An Act Of Goddo, Pretty Bad Boys, *and* Best Seat In The House. *Despite their strong following in live performances, Goddo never quite made it to the top echelons of Canadian rock.*

MUSICAL STYLE:
Rock

WHERE ARE THEY NOW?
After the band broke up, Godovitz took a breather from the fast-paced rock-and-roll world. He currently sells audio equipment. He has played the occasional gig using the Goddo name but without the other members. Godovitz has also been writing songs since the band's demise. However, in early 1989, he, Inglis, and Scarpelli began rehearsing for a comeback and lined up a number of gigs. Scarpelli has been playing in a number of Toronto groups in the meantime while Inglis has provided the drumming for The Blushing Brides.

QUOTABLE QUOTE:
Godovitz says its difficult to summarize all the highlights from the band's career, but one gig did stand out: "I think the biggest thrill of my life was when we were backstage at the Gardens playing the Max Webster New Year's Eve show and my overture was on. And they (the audience) all lit matches. I've been there so many times... sitting in amongst the people doing that... and looking through and seeing that sea of light, I thought 'Gee, we've arrived. No matter what happens from this moment on it could never get any better than it was at that moment.'"

FABULOUS FACT:
Although the band and particularly Godovitz had a reputation as wild guys and party animals, Godovitz in private life is very different. He likes to spend time with his family and enjoys listening to classical music. He says he's changed a lot from his band days and was never happy in the role as the arrogant angry young man who would do just about anything on stage to get a rise from people.

the coffee houses and bars that dotted the west and the prairies through to the east where the most evident local scene was cross-pollinating folk, rock, country, pop, and R&B. Many performers who had governed Yorkville and the larger Canadian music scene in the late '60s and early '70s wandered south for greener money and more immediate opportunity. Neil Young, David Clayton Thomas (Blood, Sweat and Tears), The Band, Andy Kim (a Montreal Boy who later struck fame writing for the Archies), Gino Vanelli, and Leonard Cohen, our quintessential poet laureate and first original performance artist. Actually, Cohen was interesting because he was not really what you call a singer or performer, yet his words carried a weight and depth that caught your attention anyway. I can recall studying Joni Mitchell and Leonard Cohen alongside Yeats and Shelley in English Literature class. I thought it was such a progressive thing at the time to be actually analyzing our own songwriters instead of the constant bombardment of everyone else's cultural content.

In Montreal at the time, bands were either emulating The Beatles or The Rolling Stones. If you liked dirty and rough music, then you would dress and sound as they did; if you preferred the clean and simple look and sound, you would do your Beatles act. Apart from The Guess Who, there were very few others to steer there attention away from the British and American influence at the time.

And yet, no one has survived the changing musical milieu as well as another of our essential poets and visionaries, Bruce Cockburn. Cockburn is a person who has managed to evolve into an artist with a global perspective and yet still remain firmly rooted in his own cultural upbringing. His early life included a stint as a street musician in Paris and a round at formal musical education at the Berkley School of Music. Although he is primarily known as a solo performer, he had also played with some local bands — Children and Three's A Crowd, to name a few. Managed by Bernie Finkelstein, who was also instrumental in the developing of earlier recording acts Kensington Market and The Paupers, Cockburn was signed to the True North label where he has released 18 albums to date. Images of mysticism and spirituality have always been pervasive in his work, but, in recent years, his political reflections on the world have brought him recognition abroad as well as respect and criticism in his own country. When I ask contemporaries about the men they think were influential in this country, Cockburn is a name that always comes up, and I think that is because he continues to grow and change with or without the approval of the industry.

I'm not one of those people that warms to the thought of my early years as a teenager. Not that I'm that old, it's just that I don't remember many great memories. I hated being a teenager. I couldn't wait to grow up

BLAST

3'S A CROWD

BACKGROUND:
3's A Crowd formed in western Canada in the mid-'60s as a Peter, Paul, and Mary-style folk trio with a splash of comedy in its act. Initial members were guitarists Brent Titcomb and Trevor Veitch and vocalist Donna Warner, all westerners who met in Vancouver in 1964.

CLAIMS TO FAME:
The group blended Second City-Style comedy with its music with Titcomb usually playing the funny man. Eventually, it began working across western Canada, and, in 1965, moved to Toronto. After regular TV appearances, 3's A Crowd signed a record deal and cut single "Bound to Fly" in New York. As folk music lost popularity, it added electric guitars and drums and members – drummer Richard Patterson, formerly of Ottawa's Esquires, and folk singer David Wiffen. Several bass players sat in, including Ken Koblun, who played with the Buffalo Springfield. It later recorded the LP "Christopher's Movie Matinee" in Los Angeles, in 1966 and was named best folk group in Canada and the country's best folk-rock group in 1967. In mid-1968, Colleen Peterson of Peterborough took Warner's place and Veitch and Titcomb left. The group later added Bruce Cockburn and Dennis Pendrith before splitting in 1969.

MUSICAL STYLE:
Folk, rock

WHERE ARE THEY NOW?:
Titcomb became a singer-songwriter, regularly appeared on TV and at folk festivals around North America, and released two solo LPs. He now performs jingles and plays folk music. Warner is office manager and singer at an Edmonton recording studio. Veitch has lived in the US since 1973, where he worked with folk singer Tom Rush, played in various bands, and worked his way into session work in California. He has played on records by Pink Floyd and Donna Summer, to name a few, and has written or co-written many songs. Peterson lives in Nashville where she's a country music singer; she released her first LP in 10 years, "Basic Facts". Patterson is a music consultant and producer for an Ottawa radio station. Wiffen is a bus driver in Ottawa. Cockburn is still a major force on the music scene.

QUOTABLE QUOTE:
Titcomb has no doubts about the group's early roots: "I guess you could say I was like Paul Stookey, Donna was Mary Travers, and Trevor was our Peter Yarrow. We were a Peter, Paul and Mary model. We'd run on stage holding hands and the whole bit."

FABULOUS FACT:
After 3's A Crowd, Titcomb and Veitch wrote songs that would win wide acclaim. Titcomb penned "Sing High, Sing Low" for Anne Murray, and Veitch co-wrote "Gloria" for American Laura Branigan.

and make adult decisions. Now, I just want to be five years old again, holding the world in the palm of my hands. Most memories, however, are connected to flashes of a musical nature, like hiding in a remote corner of the dining room behind the couch with my Woolco special transistor radio, listening to the Top 40 countdown, stifling my urge to sing at the top of my lungs. Later, in high school, I hung out with a guy who was not only five years older but a long-haired musician to boot. It seemed as if they were always going off to play another small-town Ontario summer resort, or a high school dance. In cafeterias and gyms around this province, the smell of sweat and food would mingle with the sound of rock 'n' roll or rhythm and blues. There you could hear great bands such as the Mandala, Foot in Coldwater, Lighthouse, Edward Bear, Leigh Ashford or Rhinoceros. Although they may not have had a nation of screaming teenagers screaming about them or emulating their style of playing or dressing, they were definitely part of the "mosaic" of culture in this country.

In the middle to late '70s and early '80s, the doors of liberation opened up sufficiently to let the tide of pop, acid rock, and disco up on our shores. Gino, your time had finally come! America had Elvis and his sexy stuff, but Gino was our libido King. In retrospect, I realize that I listened to more Canadian music than I imagined. The year was 1974, an enlisted college student, I grooved to the black influenced feel of "People Gotta Move", Vanelli's first single from his second album, *Powerful People*. The success of that album lead to touring in the US, opening for Stevie Wonder and Gladys Knight and the Pips. I was not surprised to learn that his most favourable response came from the black dominated audiences where he opened. His music contained the essential elements of sex, tension, and soulful passion. With the collaboration of his brother, Joe, and later Ross, these Montreal boys went on to record several other successful albums: *Storm At Sunup* (1976) and *Brother To Brother* (1978). It was shortly after that that he changed record companies and took some time to rethink. He released another album in 1981, *Nightwalker*, but not to quite the same reaction as the others. Like most musicians, he had reached a period of change and his change did not coincide with the musical tastes of the industry. It happens all the time. Just because the audience thinks you're great, it doesn't mean the people who give you the money to make the record do.

So it is the middle to late '70s and sexual liberation politics are starting to swing. Acid Rock and Heavy Metal bands are in. We are a couple of years away from another wave from the US, new wave. In the meantime, back in this country it's bands, bands everywhere. Groups such as Streetheart, Chilliwack, Mahogany Rush, Loverboy, Goddo, Tropper, April Wine, Moxy come out of the bar circuits in this country. As individuals, they did not stand out; the image of the

Moxy: look-a-like heavy rockers

band, very much remains as a band, although I'm sure that there are thousands of young boys playing air guitar and moving like Geddy Lee (Rush) or Rik Emmett (Triumph).

One of the most popular groups to be made up of experienced bar band musicians is Vancouver's Loverboy. Before forming Loverboy, Paul Dean (guitarist) and Matt Frenette (drummer) had come together via a gig with Streetheart, a popular band out in the prairies, who had also recorded several albums. Mike Reno, the vocalist in the group, came with the experience of working in Moxy and Hammersmith. He and Paul Dean began to write together and, with the guidance of their manager, Lou Blair, they approached Bruce Allen, who was also managing Bachman Turner Overdrive, Prism and, later, Bryan Adams. In 1981, Loverboy released their self-titled debut LP with much acclaim. Their appearances on US TV shows such as *Solid Gold*, coupled with touring in opening spots for Kiss and ZZ Top, would earn them the attention they needed to push themselves into the limelight. Within the first months, the album appeared on the influential Billboard chart and they had successfully launched a career that has continued until 1988 when the band broke up to pursue solo projects. The images they've chosen to show their lyrical interpretation in videos are not sexist, (it's such a limited word), but you do get the impression that most of the women they've met are beautiful, brainless bitches unworthy of anything more than decoration. Makes you wonder how men who have travelled the world several times over could have met this particular breed of woman. It seems to have worked. Loverboy has sold millions of records and influenced a generation of up-and-coming Canadian rockers.

The '80s has seen a surfacing of many talented bands in the last eight years, many of them with more women than ever. In the '60s and '70s, it was generally assumed that most of the bands or artists were male except for maybe Anne Murray; but now it seems entirely possible that men and women can work together, writing and producing music that gets recorded and finally heard on radio.

But this is also the time of solo artists for this country, of which the next two are the most identifiable as our legitimate pop stars. Legitimate in that they have the record sales as well as the popular teenage vote. Both of these men have had one of their records reach diamond (1 million records sold) status, which in a country of 10 million people is rare.

Corey Hart, an upper middle-class Montreal boy, had career origins not unlike those of Paul Anka. Corey exploded onto the music scene with the success of his single "Sunglasses at Night", which in typical Canadian fashion, broke in the US, hitting the Billboard Top 10, before causing its hysteria here. Corey had been making his way into record company offices for years. As a teenager, he had travelled to New York, visiting publishers and record companies, showing his material, hoping for interest. Opportunity came in the form of a meeting with a saxophone player from Billy Joel's band who was impressed with his songs. A late night session at which Billy Joel was a witness turned out the demo that would land him his deal with Aquarius Records, the largest Montreal independent label. And, in turn, a distribution deal with Capitol Records was struck, and on the path he continues.

Hart, more than any other recent popular image in Canada is a "pop" star in every sense of the word. Whereas off-stage he seems painfully shy and lost in serious thought, onstage he uses the periphery of

BLAST

LIGHTHOUSE

BACKGROUND:
Lighthouse, founded by Skip Prokop, who had played with The Paupers and Paul Hoffert, gained critical and popular acclaim internationally in the late '60s and early '70s with their blend of rock, orchestral music, and big band sounds. Many of Canada's top musicians, including singer Bob McBride, and Howard Shore (who later was musical director for the TV show Saturday Night Live, *were in the band. Prokop now lives in Brampton, and Hoffert lives in Toronto. A number of other members still live in and around Toronto.*

CLAIMS TO FAME:
Some of Lighthouse's biggest hits were "Hats Off To The Stranger", "Pretty Lady", "Sunny Days", "One Fine Morning", and "Take It Slow". They recorded several albums, won Juno awards, and recorded a rock ballet with the Royal Winnipeg Ballet. They were one of the first Canadian groups to tour throughout the country rather than just playing the big cities.

MUSICAL STYLE:
Orchestral, big band rock

WHERE ARE THEY NOW?:
After leaving Lighthouse, Prokop recorded some solo work and produced. He was the host of a Christian and contemporary rock show at Brampton radio station CFNY for three years; he also worked there in radio sales. He is currently a creative consultant and account executive with Marr Reynolds Advertising Inc. In late 1988, he was working on a Lighthouse greatest-hits album deal and was hoping that that would lead to the release of some of Lighthouse's live material. Hoffert has been the executive producer of the Gemini Awards, and writes commercials and film scores. Many of the other Lighthouse members continue in music. The band reunited at Ontario Place a few years ago, and Prokop doesn't discount the possibility of another performance in the future.

QUOTABLE QUOTE:
Prokop on the lack of recognition Lighthouse has received from the music industry: "I know it's going to sound like sour grapes, but I guess Paul Hoffert and I together realize that in many respects, man, we were absolute innovators. It would have been nice to have at least received some kind of merit recognition for that. If for no other reason than my kids could say, 'Gee, that was my dad.'"

Hoffert on his Lighthouse days: "It was a kind of movement and a kind of hope, an optimistic look at what society might become. It might have been naive, but it gave me a lot of good moments."

FABULOUS FACT:
Prokop credits part of his drumming success to his background in military marching bands as a high school student. He was offered a scholarship to West Point Academy in the US but turned it down for rock 'n' roll. He first met his associates at the advertising firm where he works, Daniel Marr and Doug Reynolds, as a teenager in the drum corps.

the stage as if it were a wall between him and his audience that he is trying desperately to tear down. He runs from corner to corner, climbing up onto the PA stacks, calling out to the people in the back row. Corey controls what you see in him, leaving you to wonder what is behind those slightly sleepy, very sexy eyes. Is it a hurtin' man or an angry rebellious youth who never names the reason for his anger? Not that nice upper-middle class white boys don't hurt or get angry, but maybe he doesn't want you to know that all those years of pushing demos around and being turned down hurts.

Much of the press makes reference to Corey's James Dean persona: his pout, his intense shyness, and the scores of fainting teenagers. Having done his share of TV show appearances and in-store record signings, Corey is without a doubt his own best salesman. Now, as he has come to a critical crossroad in his life, to which place will he make his transition. The release of "First Offence" (1983) found Hart touring the States, opening for similar look-and-sound-alike Rick Springfield and Hall and Oates. He quickly capitalized on his teen-idol status by working his pretty boy with a pout image — an image that has worked for and against him. Just before he hit big with "Sunglasses", in Canada, I sat on a panel with him at an independant record conference. He struck me then as very sincere and shy, but someone not to be underestimated in the ability to capitalize on anything it would take for him to make it to the top.

His second album, *Boy in the Box* (1985), parachuted him into a blue sky of success. In his own words, it seemed as if he could do no wrong. By this point, the media machines were doing their positive stuff, sell-out crowds were generating astonishing figures in merchandising revenue, and single after single went gold. The inevitable reward was the acclamation of diamond status. He wasn't the first; Bryan Adams had preceded him of late; but it was nothing to balk at. It was his third album that would ultimately change the way others saw him and the way he saw himself. *Fields of Fire* (1987) was released without much fanfare. Although it went on to sell 300,000 records, the press and industry treated it as though he had failed or lost his magic. We do that to our icons: build them up to tear them down.

In temperament, Bryan Adams is almost the exact opposite of Corey Hart, a confident (although some people I know find him arrogant), unpretentious rocker who reached

Edward Bear: impressionistic songwriters

right into the soul of Middle America in the same way that John Cougar Mellencamp does. Maybe "Kids Wanna Rock" isn't what you'd call a socially conscious song. But taken on its merits, it does connect with its youthful audience. Early in his career, Bryan was criticized for looking and sounding too much like Bruce Springsteen, but it would be wrong to think that he (or his manager, Bruce Allen) set out to exploit that connection. Rather, Adams comes right out of the bar band/hard rock tradition, the same breeding ground that gave us Springsteen, so it's no wonder, however, that if he's satisfied with being part of that tradition, and there's someone already around that does it as well as Bruce does, how Adams can ever completely escape from that shadow? And can he do anything that's completely new? And will he be remembered 20 years from now like Bruce undoubtedly will? I doubt it.

We Canadians have this tendency to compare many of our artists with their American counterparts. This is most likely because we do not have someone that is uniquely our own. Bryan Adams is like a younger version of Bruce Springsteen, Corey Hart is similar to Rick Springfield, Loverboy is like any other boy band out of the States that plays medium rock...and the list goes on. In general, we face comparison to the States no matter how talented we are. Even in Europe, where many Canadian bands have broken into the record market, they still assume we have the same political, social, cultural values as the United States of America. The poor second cousin, who keeps trying. We do have performers that are unique: The Band was one, Joni Mitchell is another, Bruce Cockburn and Gordon Lightfoot, too. Most of them seem to have emerged from the folk and country rock tradition, and common ground is their use of narrative – again, the sense of place that comes through the broad expanse of the music, that makes me think of Canada. And then there are performers like Charley Panagoniuk, a hugely popular Eskimo Indian who sings music that is a cross between Innuit and Country. Or in days gone by, from Nova Scotia, Wilf Carter, a distinctive guitarist with a flat-picking style that influenced many musicians in this country including Ian Tyson. And the chanteurs and song raconteurs of Quebec who have their own industry within their province that extends the reaches of it's impact to Europe. Or the Acadian jigs of the Eastern provinces. And now in Toronto, the West Indian and Caribbean influences of the transplanted soca and reggae music that another generation of people of colour are mixing with their experience here in Canada. All this uniquely Canadian music, however, is unlikely to be heard on the airwaves. Why? Because we follow the radio format or Top 40 and the "solid gold" stations from none

Saga: arena-size rock 'n' roll

other than our good friend, Uncle Sam. In a country where most of the radio programmers would prefer the Canadian content regulation not exist and most of them stop when they've reached their quota. No more and no less. And so the question of influential male or even female performers in this country is only relative to whether or not you believe we have an industry that is our own or now since free trade has made us the 51st state, whether or not we will have any culture that is uniquely our own.

I have not talked much of the musical influence of French-speaking Quebeçois or of Vancouver and the Prairies for I am not as familiar with those people; but, it unnerves me that, in a country so large and with so much black-influenced music, I am not able to find influential black musicians to mention. Oh, they are there to be sure; but, in the context of mainstream music, one must search thoroughly to find the people to mention. And so to me, the measure of influence has nothing to do with record sales or how many screaming teenagers adore you, or even how long you've been around these dusty parts. Someone once said "You know how influential you've been by the number of people running around immitating you." It is a rare breed of animal that would chose this profession as a lifestyle. There is no security, no dental plan, no OHIP coverage, and worst of all you can't collect unemployment insurance or disability pension. And yet we cast our dreams out into the world and trust that somewhere out there our songs will resonate with someone. And then we do it all again. In one of his songs, Bruce Cockburn writes: "All the Diamonds in this world that means anything to me. Are conjured up by wind and sunlight sparkling on the sea".

I guess fame and influence are a relative thing, a close relative to beauty – which is in the eye of the beholder.

Lorraine Segato, lead singer for Toronto's Parachute Club, is working on a solo album.

6
SIRENS OF THE NORTH

by Juan Rodriguez

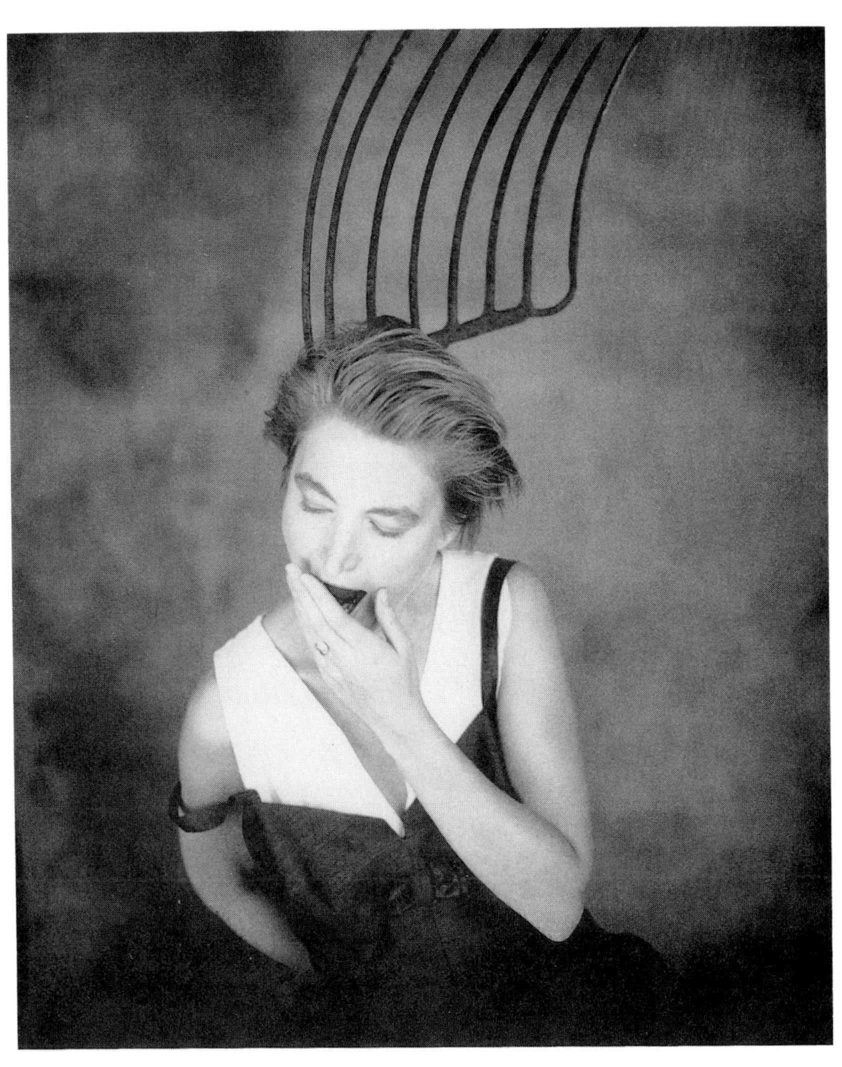

Jane Siberry: dream weaver

April 1971: The press kits are piled neatly on a table near the door of the Salle Huronite in Montreal's Chateau Champlain hotel. Inside, there's a free copy of Anne Murray's latest single, "It Takes Time", then flooding Canadian airwaves. Could this be another smash hit from the Nova Scotia gal, "the biggest headline-maker out of Springhill since 1957's mining disaster", who graced the world with "Snowbird", the first Canadian single ever nominated for a Grammy Award? There are two suitable-for-publication photos: a studio shot of Anne wearing a polka dot casual, boyish blonde hair neatly coifed, her mouth shaping cheese for the camera – she looks like the "most popular" gal in the high school yearbook – and a "candid" of Anne leaning her head on hands, gazing blankly at yet another press conference. Clippings prove she's hit the big-time: "Mel Jenkins, director of the Provincial Exhibition Association, presented a plaque to Anne Murray last night at the Prince Edward Room."

A Capitol Records bio has all you need to know: "Anne Murray is probably very much like the first girl that you ever loved. She has a simple but pretty face, a smile that comes easily and often, and eyes that can see through all the masks that you wear... She has done countless concert engagements, including appearances in Boston and Frankfurt, Germany, as a Canadian Ambassador of Goodwill... Anne has just won the Gold Leaf Award as Top Female Vocalist in Canada, which proves Capitol's feelings that 'Anne Murray sings better than just about anybody'... We can rest assured that you will give Anne all the publicity she deserves."

Anne sits alone at a long table, photographers and reporters and record people and freeloaders hovering, all promised their very own interview. Anne's most co-operative. Sitting straight on a plastic chair, she answers the same questions asked in every Canadian city she's visited since her wonderful success in the States. She rarely smiles. She

Giselle MacKenzie with Jimmy Durante: the "Hard to Get" girl

wears a pale blue blouse – real silk or polyester? – and matching brown vest and slacks, tailored like a real star's.

Here comes that nutty French-Canadian photographer, camera clicking like a machine gun. He asks Anne to do something *crazee!* She jumps on top of the piano. *Whoa!* everybody laughs. "That's where your gym training comes in handy, eh!?" She mumbles: "Yeah, I really miss it, too." Oh, Annie! Just like the slogan the record company invested for her – "Straight, clean, and simple"!

Anne Murray was the first homegrown success story produced by Capitol's Canadian subsidiary, a year after the Canadian Radio & Television Commission (CRTC) ruled that at least 30 percent of records aired in the true north strong and free must be – in some way, shape or form – Canadian. She was part of a Capitol campaign that offered a free poster of a turntable painted like a Canadian flag and gals in mini-skirts made out of the flag standing around a booth at the Canadian National Exhibition. Except for Anne, the campaign had been a flop.

A "radio personality" – stiffening up, pointing his microphone like a sabre, as if he were on TV – reveals insider knowledge about Anne recently performing without shoes. "Heh, heh Anne, what's with the barefoot image?" She says she feels more comfortable that way. She mentions that Bill Cosby recently quit to be a schoolteacher and someday she'd like to do likewise.

The "bio" concludes: "The success she has earned shows how big and far her career seems to lead...Thank you in advance for all the publicity done for our great Canadian artist."

March 1974: Anne's back, same room, same hotel, new "bio": Anne Murray was once the Snowbird lady. Now, she is that lovely "Love Song" singer..." Her first US hit since "Snowbird", it silenced restless natives who wrote her off as "overexposed".

"I was going nowhere," Anne admits. "I didn't know where I was or what I was doing." She dumped her manager and hooked up with Hollywood's Shep Gordon, who also took care of business for Alice Cooper. Within weeks, a new Anne Murray image emerged, keynoted by a photo of Annie, backstage at her Troubadour club gig in L.A., in the company of John Lennon, Alice, Harry Nilsson, and ex-Monkee Mickey Dolenz. Annie was hip. The pic made it into rock music's holy grail, *Rolling Stone*.

Today, she wears a black satin bomber jacket with drugstore-fancy embroidery, a flowery red blouse and stylish black slacks.

Question: "Last time on stage, you wore those cute little hot pants – what happened??"

Calm reply: "I used to feel insecure about my clothes. Now I have a lady who designs my outfits. It's really helped me feel relaxed and secure."

Q: "Do you ever go back to your hometown for a vacation?"

A: "Well, Springhill is not exactly a vacation town."

Does this mean she's become...Americanized?

No, she replies, she is known as a Canadian wherever she goes. She still has a house in Toronto and vacations in her motel on Prince Edward Island.

Yet, Americans seem to accept her as a legitimate stylist in her own right more than Canadians do. Why?

A: "Perhaps because Americans are more used to entertainment."

And the future? "I've gone through a lot

BLAST

SHIRLEY MATTHEWS

BACKGROUND:
Matthews, a native of the small southwestern Ontario town of Harrow, started singing in school and church. At 19, she turned her voice into a money-making hobby singing part-time while she held a full-time job in Bell Telephone's Toronto business office. She sang at high school dances in the early 1960s, and eventually graduated to the Club Bluenote. She performed with the house band and rubbed shoulders with the likes of Stevie Wonder and the Supremes, who would visit the club while playing elsewhere in the city.

CLAIMS TO FAME:
After being discovered at the Bluenote by an associate of New York producer Bob Crewe, who was handling The Four Seasons, Matthews travelled to the "Big Apple" and signed a record deal. Her biggest hit was "Big Town Boy", with lyrics that reflected her move from Toronto to New York. It sold about one million copies in 1963-64, climbed high on North American charts, and won her celebrity status. Three later tunes, "Private Property", "He Makes Me Feel So Pretty" and "Stop The Clock", had considerably less success.

MUSICAL STYLE:
Pop

WHERE IS SHE NOW?
Today, Matthews is executive assistant for a Toronto squash and racquet club, and is an accomplished squash and tennis player. She and her husband live in Unionville with their twin children, a boy and a girl. Matthews still sings at weddings and other social occasions.

QUOTABLE QUOTE:
On her decision to forsake a full-time professional music career, Matthews says, "Music was one part of my life. The other part was my family. I could have gone farther as an entertainer, but that's not to say I would be enjoying it as much as now. There is no looking back and saying 'Gee, I wish.' I've had the best of both worlds."

FABULOUS FACT:
As a singer at the Club Bluenote in the '60s, Matthews often shared the musical lineup with local acts such as David Clayton Thomas, Shawne Jackson, and members of The Mandala. All earned their musical spurs at the club, which at the time was a hotbed of home-grown talent.

these past few years and I guess I'm wiser for it. My music has changed, but I don't really think I've changed as a person...I take entertaining seriously but I don't get too wrapped up by all the other stuff, the business. The business is tough, but I'm going to have a good shot at it over the next couple of years. I'd like to do it, get it over with and then settle down and have babies or something like that...I don't want to end up like Janis Joplin. I'd like to have a voice when I'm 40..."

The Canadian way.

* * *

Juliette (Augustina Sysak) and Giselle MacKenzie were born in the same year, 1927, in the same province, Manitoba, and they most certainly did not end up like Janis Joplin.

Juliette started singing professionally as a child, making her CBC radio debut at the age of 15. Her unfettered voice offered clear comfort to Canadians during the uncertainties of World War II. She became a CBC fixture in Toronto. Three years after television's arrival in Canada in 1953, "Our Pet Juliette" became its first star. The new medium quickly made *Hockey Night In Canada* and *The Juliette Show* institutions. Live and coast-to-coast, Juliette was adopted as the nation's first force of unity for far-flung folks ("Mother, game's over, Juliette's on in a minute!").

But Juliette also faced the difficult challenge of moulding her show to fit the available time frame after the final whistle. She had only minutes to prepare a program that could last anywhere from a half hour to five minutes. How many songs could she do? Did she have time for all her guests? Who would she cut? Who got the prized duet with our pet? Canadians were fascinated by the unruffled way she handled the task. She was the perfect hostess, always reassuring in her trademark chic white blouse, tight skirt clinging — tastefully — to her curvacious figure. In the shaky early days of live TV, technical "difficulties" never fazed her. She smiled through her ordeal, never at a loss for words, elocution intact.

Her success at routinely tackling TV challenges, rarely faced by today's stars, also made her a prisoner of circumstance. By 1966 — in the midst of the irrevocable changes Beatlemania made to music and life — she got the axe, a victim of the times. Juliette was relegated to afternoon spots, servicing the few housewives not watching American soaps. Since her final cancellation in 1973, she has kept up a front —

smiling, polite, and charming — whenever she's needed for the occasional "nostalgia" interview. Canada's first shining star is virtually unknown outside the country. A trace of bitterness — tasteful — passes her lips when she maintains she has no regrets.

Although Juliette's name conjurs up nostalgia only for Canadians, millions of Americans too might remember Giselle MacKenzie. She arrived in the US in 1951, having had her fill of a few CBC radio years. By 1953, she was a regular on NBC's *Your Hit Parade*, aired Saturdays at 10:30 p.m., while Juliette waited for her cue. The new medium's version of the popular radio show (hitting the air in 1935) presented cast singers running through the week's most popular records determined by a survey — conducted by the ad agency of its sponsoring American Tobacco Company — guaranteed as "an accurate, authentic tabulation of America's taste in popular music." In 1955, MacKenzie became the show's only singer ever to perform her own hit, aptly titled "Hard To Get". (The song made the charts after she first sang it on an episode of *Justice* that dealt with the shady side of the record biz.) "Hard To Get" was her only hit, residing in the Top 40 for 19 weeks, peaking at #4.

Giselle's versatility — she could act (mainly comedy), dance, play the violin, and, above all, smile — made her a minor household name for a few years. Dinah Shore's 1956 summer replacement on *The Chevy Show* was given her own variety show in 1957. It lasted one season. After popping up alongside the likes of Bob Hope and Jack Benny, she resurfaced as Sid Caeser's TV wife on his short-lived 1963-64 comedy series comeback. She then resigned herself to a career of occasional stock appearances.

If "Our Pet" and "Hard To Get" didn't have the right stuff to inspire the dreams of the future Joni Mitchell, the distinctive voice of Sylvia Fricker did. Sylvia's quavering vocal style took root singing in the church choir directed by her music-teacher mom. She met Ian Tyson in 1959, at the age of 19, and soon became the toast of Toronto's fledgling folk scene as half of Ian and Sylvia. By 1962, they had carved a niche in New York. Two years later and married, they came up with their two most famous songs — Ian's elegiac Canadian ode "Four Strong Winds" and Sylvia's disquieting "You Were On My Mind", a huge hit for We Five in folk-rock's salad summer of 1965.

The rock era made them move to a so-so country career, eventually leading to Ian's solo career and the break-up of their marriage. Sylvia struggled painfully to find herself. It was only in 1975 that she released her first solo LP, *Woman's World,* filled with fragile feminism forced into the shadows of the freewheeling style of the Canadians she influenced most.

* * *

Liberation — fueled by burning ambition — seemed to come easy for Roberta Joan Anderson. Born in the small Alberta town of McLeod in 1943, schooled in somnambulent

BLAST

SHAWNE JACKSON

BACKGROUND:
A Toronto native, Jackson started singing in church choirs in the mid-1950s and, after playing with various groups, worked her way onto CBC-TV's Music Hop music show at age 15. She sang with Toronto band The Silhouettes before joining local soul band the Majestics, a popular showband known for its flashy clothes and energetic stage work. At one point, she was joined in the band by her brother Jay when the group was known as Shawne and Jay Jackson and the Majestics.

CLAIMS TO FAME:
After three years with the Majestics. Jackson moved on, singing with Toronto band The Stone Soul Children, before moving to the US to attend modelling school, work as a secretary, and designing clothes. In the early '70s, she recorded the perky tune "Just As Bad As You", which went Top 10 in Canada. She later cut an album and two other singles that won minor success. She was nominated for a Juno Award as Canada's most promising female singer.

MUSICAL STYLE:
Pop and soul

WHERE IS SHE NOW:
After years of singing on the bar scene, Jackson, opted for a life away from the live stage. She returned to school in 1977 to study clothes design before changing her focus to musical jingles in 1980 and later getting married. She continues to work on jingles, sings TV themes and backup for a number of Canadian artists including Christoper Ward and Luba, works in real estate, and has acted on popular TV police show Night Heat*. She hopes to have a child soon.*

QUOTABLE QUOTE:
Jackson on her private life: "I'm not on stage so what I'm doing... is privately done. I don't feel like I'm under the microscope or that I have to perform for the live *audience. I'm in charge... I'm very much a homebody."*

FABULOUS FACT:
Jackson is married to Toronto musician-songwriter-producer Domenic Troiano, who has played with the Mandala, Guess Who, Rush, and The James Gang. Troiano wrote and produced her single "Just As Bad As You", and handles the musical scoring for Night Heat*. The couple has known each other since Jackson was in her late teens.*

Saskatoon, and prepared for a cozy career as a commercial artist in Calgary's College of Art, she was ripe for the rebellion stirring inside her. She had already taught herself the ukelele and, with help from a Pete Seeger instruction disc, the guitar. She got antsy: life in western Canada struck her as too prescribed. Her voice could hardly bloom singing traditional folk songs in a Calgary coffee house called The Depression. The American folk boom – the one Sylvia was part of – reflected her craving for radical change. It was a now or never for Joan. In 1964, she split for the Mariposa Folk Festival near Toronto. She didn't return.

Her state of being free and footloose was all she needed to form her own style. "I didn't have the patience to copy a style that was already known," she later told *Rolling Stone*. While Anne Murray dutifully accepted CBC apprenticeship (on the wholesome country TV show *Singalong Jubilee*), Joni moved fast: she concocted a loosey-goosy open-tuning guitar style, and whipped up a flurry of songs based on her own experience. She made the rounds of Toronto coffee houses, got hitched to folksinger Chuck Mitchell and, little more than a year later, departed for the nearest American big-city – Detroit. Within months, she had Motown folkies in her pocket, dumped Mitchell, and answered the inevitable call from New York City.

She perfected her "look": long silken blonde hair, open face, wide eyes she seductively closed when cooing on stage, loose dresses, slinky walk. She met the right people. Her confessional songs were adapted by others. Judy Collins recorded "Both Sides Now" for the influential *Wildflowers* LP (which also introduced Leonard Cohen to the world). The song became the biggest single of Judy Blue Eyes' career (reaching #8 in 1968). In 1967, she met Elliott Roberts – who with David Geffen was signing up the counter culture's hottest singer-songwriters (including Neil Young, whose escape from Canada paralleled Joni's). David Crosby produced her first album (1967's *Songs To A Seagull*), Stephen Stills played base. Stills later wrote "Love The One You're With", anthemic of what was hyped as sexual liberation, but was traditionally known as bed-hopping.

Joni's life personified that ditty's spirit – no "Hard To Get" for her. Her songs can be summed-up: "Write about the one you're with". Her debut LP opens with "I Had A King", a self-serving (and nasty) autograph of her marriage, veiled in a "There's no one to blame…" front. She even makes mention of Mitchell's drip-dry shirts. Three LPs later, she was still picking on him in the "Last Time I Saw Richard", sniping at his bland new wife and penchant for kitchen appliances.

By 1968, she was spreading her wings on the West Coast – where all the action had shifted with the Crosby, Stills, Nash & Young crowd. Getting high on love, on themselves, on their importance in a counter-culture gone gonzo, self-indulgence ("Do your own thing") and free love were worn as badges of honour. Unlike Anne Murray, Joni was never "insecure" about what she wore…or when she took it off. Her liaisons with Graham Nash, Geffen, and James Taylor, among others, were bared for all. Taylor later expressed queasiness: "Everyone who writes

BLAST

THE POPPY FAMILY

BACKGROUND:
The Poppy Family, one of Canada's most successful musical duos, was Winnipeg native Terry Jacks and his wife, Susan (Pesklevits) of Saskatoon. They met in the late '60s while performing on the same bill at a concert in British Columbia. They began singing together under the name Powerline before marrying and becoming The Poppy Family, a name Terry found in the dictionary. They split as an act in 1970 and their marriage collapsed shortly after.

CLAIMS TO FAME:
As The Poppy Family, they released about a dozen 45s, including "Which Way You Goin' Billy" in 1969, which sold more than two million copies and went Top 5 on the influential American Billboard chart. Other hits included "That's Where I Went Wrong" and "Where Evil Grows". After splitting, Susan and Terry embarked on solo careers, and both had several successful singles: Terry with "Seasons In The Sun", which sold about 11.5-million copies in the mid-'70s, and Susan, with "Anna Marie and Evergreen".

MUSICAL STYLE:
Top 40 pop

WHERE ARE THEY NOW?:
Susan lives in Nashville with husband, Ted Dushinski, a Saskatchewan native and former Canadian Football League player; she is working on a country music career that has seen her release several singles. After a successful career as a singer-songwriter-manager-producer – and a recent comeback attempt as a singer – Terry left music in 1987 for his fervent interest in the environment. He released a new LP "Just Like That"; but, mindful of the rigors of touring, decided against the roadwork necessary to promote it. Today, he is head of a B.C.-based environmental group, and dedicates most of his time to the fight against west-coast pollution. He lives near Vancouver.

QUOTABLE QUOTE:
Terry on leaving music: "I got to thinking what more can music do for me? I had a #1 hit with the Poppy Family and a #1 hit for myself; so what would I get out of it? Another #1 hit? A bigger ranch? So what. I play "Old MacDonald" on my guitar for my daughter, but that's about it.

FABULOUS FACT:
While Terry has added the environment to his list of interests, Susan has other pursuits too. She and Ted ran a perogie and cabbage roll, Polish sausage outlet in a Nashville mall for a time. They closed it, but are looking for a new location.

songs writes autobiographical songs, but hers are sometimes alarmingly specific." Still, her confessionals linger as the most accurate reflection of an era that she, more than any other woman, helped define. It was Joni who wrote "Woodstock" ("You are me, I am you, we are what we are...We make it real"), the centrepiece of Crosby, Stills, Nash & Young's "Deja Vu" (1970) and their biggest hit ever.

It could be said that Joni Mitchell was as servile to Woodstock Nation's young bucks as Juliette was to Canada's Saturday night nationhood. But unlike "our pet", Joni exploited her role in a flattering light for all the world to see. Giselle MacKenzie never did that playing "Hard To Get".

From the early 1970s, Canadian females not only struggled under the mighty shadow of Joni Mitchell and Anne Murray's global success – and the challenge "Do this!" – but also had to face the nation's inferiority complex. Men have an easier time shedding its burden: there are more well-established male American styles to assimmilate. Caucasion Canadian women are stacked up against the glitz of Madonna, and black stars such as Tina Turner and Whitney Houston. Girl groups – an American tradition pioneered by blacks and adopted by whites when women's lib became mainstream – seemed un-Canadian. If type-casting makes the record business tick, Canadians are also resigned to being type-cast in the shadow of the world's mightiest pop culture. Thus, girlish harmony and glitz are seen as exclusively American. Copying these styles seems to be viewed as a threat to the nation's female "identity" forged by Juliette.

Ironically, Canada's largest cultural minority – Quebec francophones – asserted its sense of nationhood with ease, simply by embracing American showbiz styles and values as their own.

In 1973, Diane Dufresne's album cover depicted Quebec's reigning dive in a painted-on blue T-shirt, breasts outlined with the white fleurs-de-lis normally seen on the province's flags and licence plates, standing in an east-end Montreal alley with a gaggle of smiling street kids. Scandalous? *Pas de tout.* The cover was viewed as an adventurous, humourous, and wholesome affirmation of the sense of nationhood that flowered in the heady days before the election of the *separatiste* Parti Quebeçois in 1976.

Showbiz reigned supreme in forging a Quebeçois sense of community. As the only major French-speaking society left in North America, Quebec depended on its own star-system as a mirror of survival and growth. This star-system borrowed freely from the

Ian and Sylvia Tyson: two strong winds ▶

obsessive hustle that puts Americans in the spotlight. And women stood as equals on Quebec's stage.

It was Monique Leyrac who put "Mon Pays" (Gilles Vigneault's historic anthem) on the local hit parade, triggering stirrings of separatism in the mid-1980s. The song not only launched her career in France but reawakened the country's awareness of another indigenous Francophone culture in the world. Pauline Julien, born in France, stoked the national flame. The pair represented the intellectual side of Quebec's star system. The other side was ruled by populist singers who borrowed liberally from American styles. The most talented among them, Ginette Reno (her rotund frame housing a powerful set of pipes), was the first Quebec singer to appear on Johnny Carson's TV show (and played Vegas to boot, opening for Don Rickles). Reno had a hard time with the intelligensia at first — her style was too sentimental and overblown; but, she eventually won their respect with sheer talent.

Reno's career helped establish a new axiom in the nationalist credo: Success by any Quebecer — regardless of political leaning or musical style — should be recognized as a success for Quebec. The local press and media never missed a chance to loudly trumpet any international success by Quebecers. Language barriers don't prevent their pursuit, even if it is an exercise in futility. The people — not only fans — support them. Little wonder that when former teenage star Celine Dion — hailed in Tokyo, Paris, praised by Pope John Paul II — was ready to record an English album in 1988 (produced by Montrealer Aldo Nova), the news that she wanted to enter Madonna territory was greeted as an affirmation of the health and variety of Quebec's popular culture. Quebec loves a gamer. Thus, 36-year-old rockeuse Marjo (Morin) was adopted as an orphan after she took a chance by quitting a successful group (Corbeau) that had reached a dead end in 1986. She was broke, living with her parents or with friends, and burnt out by too many nights of hollaring and partying. She staked everything on *Celle qui va*, an album designed to expand her following from hard fans to anyone who likes catchy songs with soul. By 1988, the album had gone double-platinum (200,000 sales) after spending a year in the Top 20. The trooper in her reflected that of her people. So, when Coca-Cola offered her big bucks to do a TV commercial, she was able to say "Only on my own terms."

* * *

Back in English Canada, the shadow of Anne Murray and Joni Mitchell proved suffocating when "new wave music" (sexually ambiguous, punky, anti-formula) tried to ruffle Canadian feathers in the late 1970s. The two superstars seemed to have typecast Canadian females as either smoothly bland or

Liona Boyd and friend: ethereal and privileged

smoothly "sensitive", incapable of bruising sexuality.

The shadow's most talented victim was Carol Pope, singer and brains behind Rough Trade. Clearly, Pope offered some of the most humourous, biting, bold, brassy, campy, and cleverly ambiguous commentary on the sexual revolution heard in America. "High School Confidential", a wicked poke at teenage porn dream cliches lived out by most adolescents, and "Victim of Fashion", a textbook on the slavishness of fads, are classics that had all the makings to hit the US in a big way. But they didn't.

Martha and the Muffins fared better, but they should be remembered as more than one-hit wonders. The Toronto group's 1980 albums, *Metro Music* and *Trance and Dance* conveyed a highly melodic style that transcended their categorization as "new wave". "Echo Beach" — a huge hit in Canada and big enough in the US and England to serve as a career launching pad — defined an eclectic style: bubble-gum vocals providing an effective counterpoint to alienation, adventurous tunes contrasting off-beat changes with the best pop hooks, and an eminently listenable sound that swept you into a more haunting, disquieting mood. Perhaps the contrasts — what lurked beneath the pop-rock shimmer was the group's most interesting and attractive facet — were two subtle for the marketplace. Perhaps two lead singers called Martha (secretaries who recorded in their spare time) were not the stuff of Hip.

Meanwhile, Carroll Baker simply bowled her way onto the country music scene — claiming her style more direct than Anne Murray's "pop" crossover and doggedly working to prove so. The Bridgewater, Nova Scotia native was never shy about it, either, having first stormed the stage at age four. By 19, she was a regular on the Ontario country circuit, scoring a record contract two years later and, in 1976, signing with RCA. That year, she decided to make her Juno Award nomination (female country singer) count. Her scorching version of Conway Twitty's "I've Never Been This Far Before" on the awards show's usually-staid national telecast did the trick. Looking and sounding like a cross between Tammy Wynette and Dolly Parton, appearing older than her age, she took Toronto by storm. City slickers applauded her sassy voice and dynamism, but snickered privately over her lack of "sophistication". However, within a couple of years, she had a CBC-TV show of her own, and gave RCA bigger record sales than any of its other Canadian acts. She's had a tight lock on Canadian country since, in addition to a welcome mat in Nashville.

* * *

The most durable international career carved by a woman starting out in the '70s was that of a non-singer who played highbrow music, flung on the public in what was perceived as a desperate record company gimmick, her talents doubted because of her looks.

Liona Boyd, a classical guitarist in the Spanish style, was only 24 when her first album was released in 1974. Canadian critics were tongue-tied at best, snide and nasty at worst, when forced to evaluate her. Wasn't this record somewhat, uh, premature for someone with only two years of training from a maestro (Alexandre Lagoya), tackling a musical genre so difficult to play that only prod-

The McGarrigle Sisters: quirky folkies

igies would be unashamed to go public? And first-rate female classical guitarists were virtually unheard of, especially one with long blond hair, a pure face, and pristine dresses. Was she merely a tool of the record company? Then again, she was a *Canadian*...and she must have *guts* to take the stage...and she was *beautiful*...and how could pop critics who knew nothing about the classics, and the intricasies of the classical guitar, pass judgment?

So the public, prompted by a well-oiled publicity campaign, decided. The album sold 30,000 copies, a remarkable debut for any Canadian, astonishing for a classical musician. Surely this was a fluke, critics said, a result of a fickle, unknowing public. A blasphemy against the "real thing". They snickered when she was accompanied to a Juno Awards ceremony by Prime Minister Pierre Trudeau. The young lady was nothing but a clever opportunist!

Yet, Liona Boyd grew stronger under fire. She continued her musical studies and, undaunted, rolled out more successful albums. Her recordings became even more attractive in the crystal clear digital sound wrap of the compact disc format.

Over the years, Boyd has earned some begrudging critical respect. Her records have sold nearly a million copies worldwide. A remarkable achievement for any classical soloist.

"Remarkable" naturally springs to mind to describe Kate and Anna McGarrigle's arrival at Carnegie Hall in February, 1980. The McGarrigle sisters defy description, much like the way they've defied the rules of the game of "show business". They don't give a "show", and "business" bores them. Yet their shows are, regardless of quality, a constant reminder of the force and fragility of music's purest purpose when it is sung and played spontaneously. And, on their own terms, they've managed to take care of business quite nicely, thank you.

So Carnegie Hall was as full of paradox as the evening's headliners. Its storied past glittered despite its fusty dignity. Beautiful in a creaky way — this before renovations signalled complete by Frank Sinatra years later — the hall delivered, for the umpteenth time, the air that an event of importance was about to take place. Yet, it had the atmosphere of a 19th century farm house on Christmas Day. The McGarrigles' chipper white-haired mother attending to children of children, friends and strangers. Kate, Anna, and fellow musicians — boyfriends, mates, men they'd known for over half their lives — more in awe over Carnegie Hall's beauty than their "arrival" there, concerned about not missing the opening act (Rick Danko, fellow Canadian formerly of The Band, and Paul Butterfield, blues harmonica wizard they flocked to see in Montreal coffee houses some 13, 14 years back). Irony, too: National Film Board cameras were in place to document the event (resulting in debut film by future award-winner Caroline Leaf) — the same NFB for which Kate and Anna had, as part of the informal folk group The Mountain City Four, supplied the music for a 1969 documentary called *Helicopter Canada*.

The thing about the McGarrigles is that music is their muse, part of their lives, but far from running their lives. In 1976, they managed to put out an album so out-of-the-ordinary that critics were stunned with ecstasy (Stereo Review: album of the year; Melody Maker; rock LP of the year; New York Times: #2 pop LP), yet deemed too "uncommercial" to generate mass airplay. More irony: Anna's first song, "Heart Like A Wheel", was recorded by Linda Ronstadt for a 1974 LP bearing the same title, commercial enough to become her first #1 gold album; Kate's "The Work Song" was a highlight of Maria Muldaur's first solo album, her only gold. Warners (manufacturers of the Ronstadt and Muldaur LPs) bent the sisters' arms to follow-up with two glossier sounding records. Critics had mixed feelings, the public ignored them, and, now playing in a sold-out Carnegie Hall, they were again without a record label.

More irony: the McGarrigles first attracted heavy attention in their native land with the news that their first French song, *"Plainte pour Ste-Catharine"*, was #1 in Belgium. And more: Three years after Warners dumped them, their Canadian best-seller (appropriately titled "French Record") was judged by *Rolling Stone* as one of 1981's best albums.

When Polydor restored their cult following with 1983's "Love Over and Over" — even Dire Straits guitarist Mark Knopfler's presence failed to make it "commercial" enough — the only non-original song was a French translation of Bob Seger's "You'll Accompany Me".

All of which is a roundabout way of saying that the basic honesty of the musical process in its purest form — spontaneous emotion — is a quality that has always been, and always will be, misread, perverted or considered undesirable in the popular music industry. But don't expect Kate and Anna to be Heart's Wilson sisters. What they offer is rare: a blend of all music that blows in the wind — centuries old or brand new — concocted without artifice. It is by essence ragged, and can never be labelled "fusion" music. Their lyrics are more poetic justice than poetry. Like snow flakes, their performances are never the same.

* * *

Back in Toronto, the demise of Rough Trade and Martha & the Muffins left only Parachute Club's Lorraine Segato and avant-gardist Jane Siberry to carry the torch through the tightly formatted music marketplace of the 1980s. In their own radically differing ways, both carefully crafted their styles to the commercial exigencies of the times.

Segato is the queen bee among the trio of female singers that provide a medium of glamour to the sartorially with-it Toronto septet's image. Musically and lyrically, Parachute Club plays it as safe as the name unwittingly implies — sort of a hip *Up With People*. The 1986 album, *Small Victories*, was largely produced by John Oates and sounds as competitive as the eminently successful Hall & Oates. Plenty of cute production hooks and sonic twists, rhythms that straddle the line between soft and hard rock. Segato's earnest girl-next-door voice is well-suited to the "listen to your heart" lyricism telegraphed by the song titles: "Love is Fire", "Secret Heart (Wild Zone)", "Walk to the Rhythm of your Heartbeat", "Love and Compassion". The title song's chorus offers a cozy exhortation worthy of a commercial jingle: "Small victories are big steps...". The same slogan follows the lyric sheet's comfortable political "statement" reassuring one and all that Parachute Club is against South Africa and for the North American Indian.

Jane Siberry is more adventurous, the first Canadian to mine turf excavated by performance artist Laurie Anderson, the post-modern poet laureate who managed to carve a small niche on the US charts. Siberry, blonde and suitably ascetic, lightens up the style for wider acceptance by legions of fans intrigued by other worldly New Age styles. Weird but not way-out, spooky but not threatening, her glacial voice is matter-of-fact without being too expressionless. Her first album, *No Borders Here* (1984) and *The Speckless Sky* (1985), gave her the sort of hard-core cult fans who bask in the discovery of something never heard before that may just be important. She broke through to the other side — where the cash register is — on 1987's *The Walking*, which got her a story and review in *Rolling Stone*. Recorded digitally to give the echoes and crystal musical fillips a Windex shine a foot deep, loaded for bear with titles-for-the-curious such as "The White Tent The Raft", "Lena Is A White Table", and "The Bird In The Gravel", the album represents Siberry's well-conceived strategy to capture the not-inconsiderable mainstream audience of people with the time and inclination to explore the canyons of their minds and listen for the sounds of silence. This is a perfect soundtrack for a marketplace that transcends boundaries of nations...as well as airplay formats.

More than any other Canadian, including Siberry, Rita MacNeil personifies the battle of pure voice against the rampent categorization that — while always a part of the record industry — is a confused schizoid plague inherent in Canada's geo-political spot in the shadow.

Her powerful voice, by turns, soars like an angel — sweet and vulnerable — and digs in like a fighter prepared to go the distance, tough and low-down. But the voice has always faced an uphill battle against those who judge a book by its cover and what shelf

Lorraine Segato: fresh-faced girl-next-door

to place it on. MacNeil is short and fat, and middle-aged. She's a small-town Maritimer (make that "village" — Big Pond, Cape Breton, pop. 176). She sings folk music — read: no commercial potential. When she attempted to consolidate the modest success of her breakthrough 1987 album (which found airplay on middle-of-the-road stations) with the glossier, rockier *Reason to Believe* a year later, critics howled "sell-out".

It was a long time coming. Twenty-five years before she first attracted national attention at the age of 43, Rita MacNeil had left Nova Scotia for Toronto, convinced that her talent would take her places. Sylvia Fricker was her age and she making it on the folk scene. But Rita never made it beyond the Mariposa festival and the Riverboat coffee house — except to Eaton's as a clerk and into richer homes as a cleaning woman. Two kids, a busted marriage and baker's dozen years later, she returned home to people who'd always give her a listen. In 1986, she was chosen to play 88 shows in six weeks at Vancouver's Expo — no doubt one of those token choices Canada's cultural commissars make to show off the nation's "cultural music" to the world. As usual, it took tourists smitten by the Voice to alert the hosts to the treasure in their midst. A year later, *Flying on Your Own* began its way to platinum sales in Canada. The title track, an ode to women's liberation, was adopted by Toronto feminists and helped win her a 1987 Juno for "most promising female vocalist". It was recorded by none other than Anne Murray (winner of the same prize nearly 20 years previous). Yet even Annie had less success than Rita getting it on the radio. The song "got terrific response from live audiences", Murray said to *Maclean's* in '88. "It died for one reason: it is written from a woman's point of view — and all radio programmers are men. I don't have much time for people like that, but that's the way it is in this business."

MacNeil, who finally had enough money in 1987 to buy a house nearer Sydney's airport, accepts the accolades with a grain of salt and "The Music's a Going Round Again", a let-bygones-be song connecting 25 years of bitter and now sweet experience in Toronto: "And this is where my song began/I tried to hold you, you weren't ready then."

And what of Anne and Joni at the dawn of

their third decade in the business? Their careers have stabalized. Having reaped their largest harvests, they put their established images on automatic pilot. It would be another seven years before they'd see another Canadian woman crack the US market with a bang.

Anne Murray was now one of the world's most popular purveyors of the middle road, at home with soft-pop or country-ballads. In 1976 – two years after Hollywood management ran out a brief string of minor hits and three Top 40 albums (*Country* going gold) – Annie took her promised sabbatical. One last time to figure out a career plan that would stick and allow her to have a second child.

"What had happened," she said serenely in 1979, seven months pregnant, "was that although we'd signed with Shep Gordon, we weren't being managed by him. We were getting someone in his office. So we figured if we approached it right, we could do it ourselves. I couldn't have done it without learning from the Americans. That's the trouble with the Canadian music industry. They sit on their asses here and wait for it to happen. When you're talking showbiz, you're talking Los Angeles and New York, and you've got to go there to make it. You can't sit around."

So, while she greased the wheels for the push to finally put her over the top for good, she went to the bank. Anne Murray became the TV voice and image of the Bank of Commerce (the only bank in Springhill when she opened her first account as a kid). The ads were enormously successful on both sides of the wicket, "like little works of art". The cash flowed, and so did sales of albums and singles "*Let's Keep It That Way*"(1978), over a million sales; "*You Needed Me*", her first US #1 song.

Joni Mitchell's music became more sophisticated, her lyrics less sophomoric (*Hejira* and *Don Juan's Reckless Daughter* are probably most enduring). The string of gold records stopped when fans caught on that her fling with jazz was for real: the widely hyped LP of Charles Mingus compositions, given his blessing as he was dying; a live fusion-jazz set, *Shadows And Light*, with genre stars Pat Metheny and Jaco Pastorious. She liked this so much she directed a movie of it. In 1982, she tackled aging in Wild Things Run Fast. She began painting full-time.

In 1984, she returned with *Dog Eat Dog*, produced by synthesizer whiz Thomas Dolby. The critics ate her up as a sell-out, fans didn't buy, Joni went into self-exile. Four years later, she tried again with *Chalk Mark in a Rain Storm*, an attempt at reconciling new technology with her old style, adorned with some socio-political songs (a must in the era of so-called renewed rock "conscience"). The press tour and the interviews in major magazines got Joni into print. "*Chalk Mark In A Rain Storm*" raced up the charts for a month, stalled after breaking Number 30, then died. Not enough sales to warrant the concert tour used to support the record. Joni Mitchell had taken her place as a minor casualty of changing times in the record market.

By 1986, big company talent scouts and agents scratched their heads in a seemingly futile search for the first Canadian female to catch the world's imagination in fifteen years. The trouble is, they'd already passed on her.

She was born in an Alberta town smaller than Joni Mitchell's (Consort: pop. 650). She'd dabbled in "performance art", crawling on stage in a garbage bag or as part of a seven-hour reenactment of plastic heart surgery. In 1983, she started performing something that's now labelled "punkabilly" or what she calls "torch and twang". By 1988, she was the new queen of country music, with such wide appeal that *Rolling Stone* critics voted her best new female singer.

But not before all record execs turned down k.d. lang's bid for an American recording contract – except one: Seymour Stein, head of Sire Records, whose biggest star was Madonna. After he first saw the sassy girl with the neo-crew cut and campy country skirts as an opening act at New York's Bottom Line Club in 1985, Stein boldly told her: "You are what country music would have been if Nashville hadn't screwed up." k.d. (kathy) didn't need convincing: "I'm going to change country music," she stated flatly.

The day after April Fool's, 1987, she played the Roxy, on Sunset Strip, Hollywood. *Variety* sealed its approval: "k.d. lang thrilled and delighted with 21 ace-perfect tunes... She and her terrific band polka'd, vamped, swung, and rocked, bringing new meaning to 'New Country'." *Los Angeles Times:* "k.d. IS A-OK – A star is born."

k.d. lang has turned the world of country music topsy-turvy – Nashville has never seen or heard anyone like her – because she's a study in role reversal. Starting with a man dedicated to this switcheroo: "Stand by your woman."

When Larry Wanagas, an independent manager from Edmonton, resorted to the want ads for a singer to front a "Texas swing, twin fiddle band" in 1982, little did he know that katherine dawn lang was his ticket to a magnificent obsession. Her tiny prairie hometown was about the only country in her: she studied classical piano, took up folk guitar, got into rock music by reading her older sister's *Rolling Stone*, dabbled in then-trendy "performance art" (having no doubt read of Laurie Anderson in the *Stone*) and, at age 20, answered Wanagas' ad by telling him she wanted to be a jazz singer. Wanagas talked her out of that and set about finding the right vehicle for the powerful, versatile voice in a body that couldn't stop twitching. "Cowpunk" was born.

He worked her on Canada's alternative music circuit – college stages, rock clubs – as well as traditional country bars. The idea was a renewal of rich traditional country music values (which had been buried by slick crooners and harmony groups sounding like they came out of Las Vegas), complemented by an amplified, rock 'em-sock 'em sound suited to the eclecticism of Western swing (influenced by '30s jazz and polka tempos). kathy was a quick study. Her reputation grew just as fast – a wacko, spellbinding singer and kinetic performer. She turned

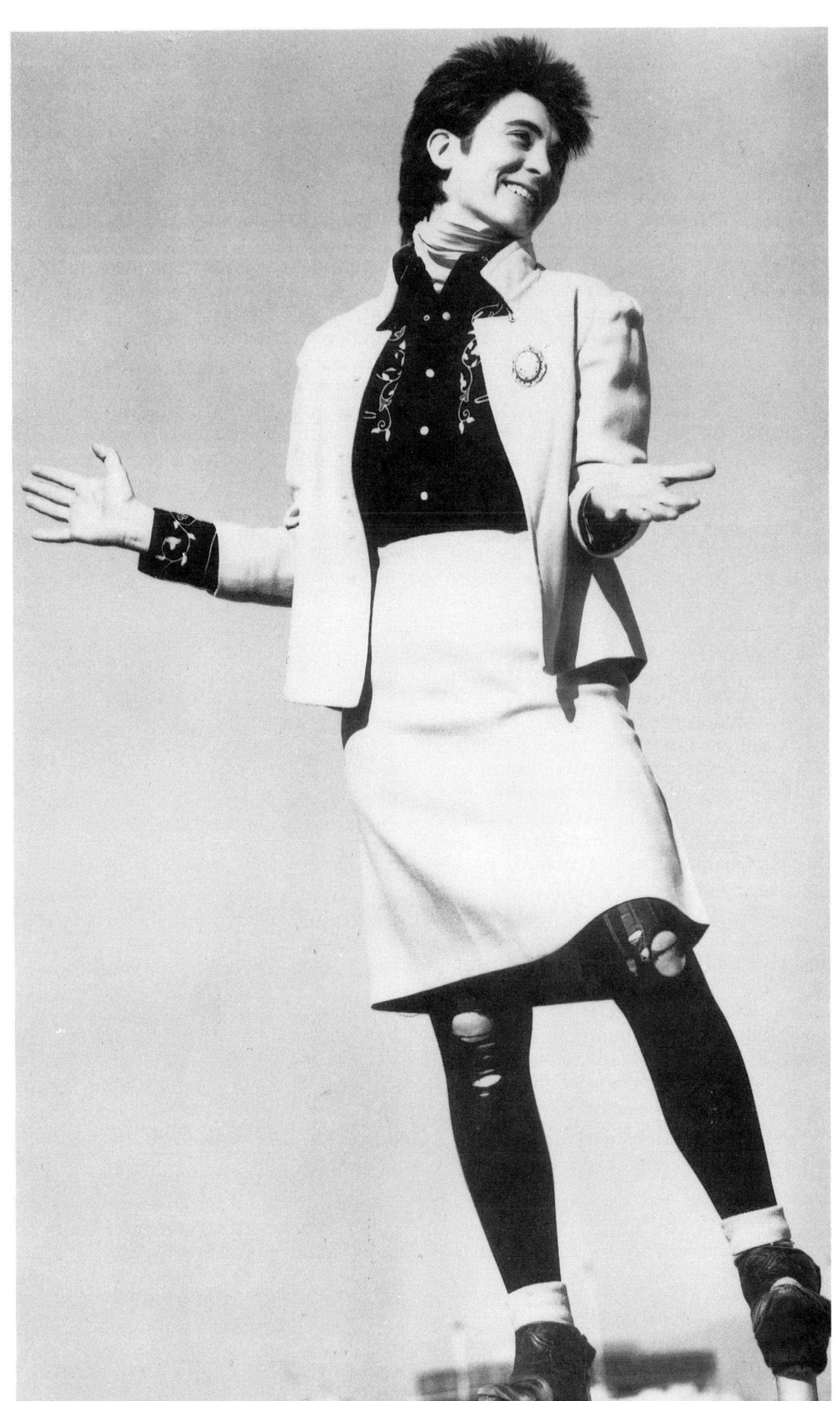

k. d. lang:
the cowpunk original

on young urban Canucks, who thought country was nothing but Tommy Hunter, the Carter family or the Oak Ridge Boys. Big-city reviewers took note. The *The Globe and Mail* saw her as a cross between Olive Oyl and Elvis Costello. Her voice eerily recalled Patsy Cline's, with the added supple seduction of Peggy Lee.

When Wanagas was given the cold shoulder by Canadian disc men, he spent $8,000 producing her first album, *A Truly Western Experience*, for his Indie Bumstead label. All that netted her was a 1985 Juno award for Most Promising Female Singer. Wanagas kept plugging, finally landing a second bill at the Bottom Line. The bottom line was Sire's Stein. Goodbye small-budget album and hello rock revivalist producer Dave Edmunds (lang's second choice when Elvis Costello wasn't available). Stein committed himself to a hefty $150,000 budget. Trouble was Edmunds refused to produce outside England and demanded $75,000 pay. So k.d. lang and the Reclines crossed the great divide, and spent three months locked up with Edmunds, who got her wound up on edge because of his rule of using first takes (for their now or never spontaneity). Despite their discomfort with the old country's "backward" standard of living and what lang grudgingly calls a "learning experience" with Edmunds, $250,000 later, the result was *Angel With A Lariat*. k.d. was the new sweetheart of the rodeo.

The album sounds rich and natural, a modern approach to country roots, with a powerful kick to boot. Its accessibility to country neophytes is similar to the Rolling Stones' approach to black rhythm & blues nearly 25 years earlier. It is within this context that k.d. lang says she's going to change country music.

So, it's natural that it was only after she appeared on TV's ultra-hip *Late Night with David Letterman* that she was invited to appear on *Hee-Haw* and meet up with another Canadian — you guessed it — Gordie Tapp, a regular on Tommy Hunter's show before she was born. And only natural that the old madonna of country, Minnie Pearl, insisted on a duet with the country Madonna. And only natural that k.d. became the first Canadian to clean up Nashville's country music awards since Anne Murray.

And maybe, just maybe, it's only natural a story such as this was written in the great white north, where tuques are required garb for winter tours.

Juan Rodriguez has been a rock critic and sports columnist for a variety of Montreal publications.

7
MASSAGED BY THE MEDIA

by Dan Hill

Liberty Silver: underrated and ignored

n 1976, I won a Juno award for Most Promising Male Vocalist. The night itself was something of a disaster for me. I'd been slated to perform live-to-track (a process in which I play my guitar and sing live to a pre-recorded tape) my first (and, at the time, only) hit single in Canada. My performance turned out to be dreadful. The playback wasn't loud enough. All I heard was my voice, swimming in so much reverb that my head was spinning. To make matters worse, the drums didn't appear until half-way through the song. I was so alternately far behind or so far in front of the beat that I might as well have been singing "My Boyfriend's Back (and There's Gonna Be Trouble)".

More than a million Canadians saw me perform that night for the first time. I wore my manager's oversized courduroy pants and my best friend's crumpled purple turtleneck, a dreadlock hairstyle that predated Tracy Chapman's by 12 years and white gym socks. No shoes. I wasn't quite the grand manipulator of image that David Bowie was; let's face it, Canadian pop music in 1976 wasn't exactly reeling in visual slickness. But that night the germ of my image was born. The next morning my performance was cited as the low point of the awards by Blaik Kirby of the Toronto *Globe and Mail.* He referred to my voice as "unbeautiful" and my song, "You Make Me Want To Be", as an unwitting parody of a pop song. I left my apartment the next day deeply embarrassed. I was convinced that people would point at me, smirking. Instead, more people stopped me for autographs than ever before. Apparently, winning a Juno award mattered more than my weak performance — or a negative review.

It didn't take me long to realize the power of the media to influence the public's attitude toward pop music. On the basis of one award show, my first album went from being a moderate hit to a best seller almost overnight.

My early attitudes toward the Canadian

BLAST

STREETHEART

BACKGROUND:
The band formed in Regina in 1976, combining members of western Canada groups The Great Canadian River Race and the second version of Witness Inc. Original Streetheart members were singer Kenny Shields, bassist Ken "Spider" Sinnaeve, and keyboard player Daryl Gutheil from Witness and drummer Matt Frenette and guitarist Paul Dean from River Race. When personality clashes led to the departure of Dean and Frenette, guitarists John Hannah and later Jeff Neill and drummer Bob "Herb" Ego were added. The group split in 1984 after failing to break into the U.S. market.

CLAIMS TO FAME:
After gaining a solid reputation on the western Canada bar circuit, Streetheart moved to Toronto in 1977, where its high-energy live performances caught the attention of fans and record companies. The band signed a record deal which led to their debut LP, Meanwhile Back in Paris, *which sold about 200,000 copies in Canada and produced three singles, "Action", "Look At Me", and "Feel It". Later LPs were* Under Heaven Over Hell, Quicksand Shoes, Drugstore Dancer, Streetheart *and* Dancing With Danger. *Other memorable Streetheart singles were a cover of the Rolling Stones tune "Under My Thumb", "Here Comes The Night", done earlier by Van Morrison, "Hollywood and Snow White". The band won a Juno Award as Canada's most promising group in 1979.*

MUSICAL STYLE:
Hard-driving rock and roll

WHERE ARE THEY NOW?
Shields has sung with two groups, most recently The Kenny Shields band, which, for a short time in the summer of 1988, included all original Streetheart members. He lives in Winnipeg, where he is looking for a record deal as a solo performer; Sinnaeve plays with Tom Cochrane and Red Rider; Gutheil still plays music around Winnipeg; Dean and Frenette went on to impressive careers with Canadian band Loverboy, which had a string of LPs and hits, including Turn Me Loose, The Kid Is Hot Tonite, *and* When It's Over. *In early 1989, with Loverboy on hiatus, Frenette was working on Dean's solo LP and considering putting a new band together with Dean.*

QUOTABLE QUOTE:
Shields says Streetheart's performances often saw band members jump into the audience. "The live act is what we're remembered for... the blood and the guts and sweat and how it was always consistent and always was a good time."

FABULOUS FACT:
In 1970, Shields' musical career was almost nixed when he was involved in a serious car accident in Saskatoon. He suffered 13 shattered bones and almost lost an arm, but after a five-year recovery, was back in business, first with a second version of Witness and later with Streetheart.

media were largely influenced by Bernie Finkelstein, who, along with Bernie Fiedler, was my manager at the time. I looked upon his pronouncements on the press or radio as gospel – to the point where frequently, before an important newspaper or magazine interview, he'd coach me on the answers I should give to certain key questions.

"Whatever you do," he'd begin, pacing restlessly and chain-smoking like some possessed fiend, "don't cut up Canadian radio. The press and radio in this country hate each other and the press would love nothing more than to get to throw a few barbs at, say, CHUM. But if you do, you may never get a new single played on their station again." Here he'd pause meaningfully waiting for the full impact of his words to sink in. *Never get a new single played again*: for an up-and-coming singer-songwriter, this was the kiss of death.

In retrospect, I think Bernie trained me to take the Canadian press too seriously. It was completely natural for Finkelstein to assume that the Canadian press would be of paramount importance to any artist he might manage; after all, the tremendous national success he'd achieved with Bruce Cockburn and Murray McLauchlan was due in part to very strong critical support from the Canadian press. But none of us really understood the truth at the time: my songs were geared more toward radio, especially – horror upon horrors – American radio. But if radio exposure is a singer's fastest ticket to success, positive press signified respectability, and acceptance from the establishment. For a manager or group who honed their craft through trial and error, the need for quasi-intellectual approval from the press can become overly important.

Interestingly enough, if the value of the Canadian press was overrated by my managers, Canadian television was vastly *underrated.* Once again, I think Finkelstein and Fiedler were influenced by their experiences with their other artists. Cockburn and McLauchlan's undeniable stage charisma didn't translate well through the medium of TV. I was warned to be wary of Canadian TV. It was a "waste of time". Supposedly it didn't sell records and often conspired to make you look stupid.

Along with my two managers, I was interviewed on a show called *The Profet Picture.* Mel Profet, a former football star for the Toronto Argonauts, was the host. The interview was going smoothly until Profet asked Bernie Fiedler why, after so many years of managing only Bruce and Murray, he'd decided to take me on as a client. Bernie, looking like the perfect manager, cleared his throat elegantly and began, "We decided to manage Dan because…" at which point he froze (later on he told me he was fantasizing about one of the female technicians

BLAST

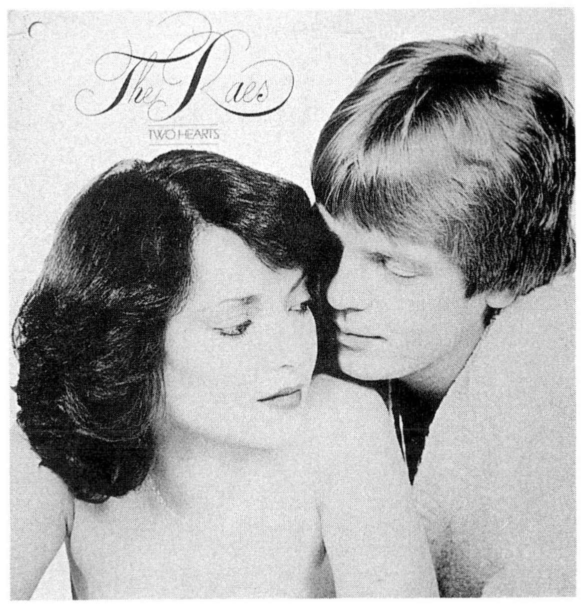

THE RAES

BACKGROUND:
Robbie and Cherrill Rae met in England when both were performing solo. Cherrill had some regional success in southwestern Ontario before that in a group The Comic Opera Rock Show. They moved to Cherrill's hometown, St. Thomas, Ont. and began performing a cabaret-style show in 1974. Their career took off in the mid-'70s when disco music became popular. The couple split in the early '80s. Robbie lives in Toronto, and Cherrill lives in Bolton, Ont.

CLAIMS TO FAME:
Their first big single was a remake of "Que Sera Sera", a song that neither of them thought would be much of a record. The song took off, and they became popular in disco circles. Other Top 10 Canadian hits were "A Little Lovin' (Keeps the Doctor Away)", and "I only Want To Get Up and Dance". The Raes were nominated for two Juno Awards. Because of their disco sound, they were once asked to be interviewed by a newspaper called Black Hollywood *because many people in the US who hadn't seen them thought they were a black act. Their success led to their own nationwide television show and tour dates in New York and Las Vegas. They were later offered a five-year television deal but turned it down.*

MUSICAL STYLE:
Disco-pop

WHERE ARE THEY NOW?:
After parting ways, Robbie had a successful solo single with "Finger On It". He continues to perform regularly at Toronto clubs, and recently has been writing songs with ex-Saga members Steve Negus and Jim Gilmour. In the fall of 1988, Robbie was on the verge of signing a joint Canadian and European album deal. Cherrill married Toronto musician Nick Cucunato. She had performed in a number of bands, Backstreet, C.C. Rae, and Rockit, and now sings with the Cherrill Rae Trio, a lounge act.

QUOTABLE QUOTES:
Robbie on the duo's decision to turn down the long-term TV contract because of the possiblity of overexposure: "Nobody's going to go out and buy your records when they can see you for nothing every week." Cherrill, on the same decision: "The record company said it would hurt our sales, but that was stupid. Look at groups that make videos today. It was the biggest mistake we ever made."

FABULOUS FACT:
The Raes might have had a Top 40 hit in the US on the Billboard chart with their song "A Little Lovin" but for a typographical error. The song was moving up the charts with a bullet, but the following week the song had dropped on the charts. Apparently, someone reversed the chart number from 39 to 93. The Raes record company was puzzled and halted all promotion of the single.

with whom he'd apparently had a torrid affair) for some 15 or so agonizing seconds – which by TV standards is a lifetime of silence. Finally, he said something to the effect of "Sorry I froze" and Finkelstein quickly picked up the slack. When the interview finished the cameramen started moving their equipment out of the room.

"Wait a minute," Finkelstein bellowed, "when are we gonna reshoot the part of the interview where my partner froze?"

"We're gonna use the entire segment" explained the director. "It was great TV when Bernie froze like that. Real human. Should come across great to the audience."

Bernie stood passively off to the side, still trying to make eye contact with the female technician. Finkelstein picked up a chair and waved it furiously over his head – he probably has the most formidable temper of anyone I've met – and started threatening law suits. But it wasn't until he swore he'd never allow any of his artists to appear on their station again that the director relented and shot the scene again.

Over the next few years I was struck by the difference in tone between American and Canadian TV interview shows. Just about every televised interview I did in Canada had a suspicious edge to it: What kind of compromises had I made in order to succeed? Wasn't I embarrassed to be singing such personal songs? I was discovering that Canadians tended to be wary of success stories, especially Canadian success stories. They were skeptical, strangely disapproving of unabashed ambition. American TV was something else altogether. I wasn't interviewed so much as celebrated; each interviewer came armed with enough chart statistics about my latest record release to start up a PR firm.

Admittedly, my background was great "American dream" fodder for any talkshow host with a vaguely jingoistic beat. That my parents were born and raised in the States and moved to Canada in 1953, due in part, to escape racial oppression (my father's black, my mother white) fascinated the US TV media. Through some twist of logic, they interpreted my sudden success in the States as a symbol that racial strife was resolved in America. One generation had fled their country; now a new generation was returning with a hit record.

If some Americans embraced me for what I symbolized to them, the Canadian public and media to an extent eventually embraced me because I was accepted by American TV. It was, alas, a magnified version of the '76 Juno award syndrome. My third album quadrupled in sales in Canada several months after its hit single, "Sometimes When We Touch", had peaked in Canada. As I wasn't touring Canada at the time; most of those sales were to Canadians impressed with my success in the US. Thousands of Canadians must have approached me after my appearance on the *Merv Griffen Show* to tell me how proud they felt to see a Canadian on such a big American show. For many of these people, it took an American show to make them feel patriotic toward a Canadian singer. Even more ironic was the brief conversation I had with Merv Griffen during a rehearsal before his show. He kept pulling at the waist of his Adidas sweat pants as he talked. That's right: Merv in sweats.

"I heard a tape of one of your Canadian concerts. They really like you up there don't they?"

"Ah-yeah-I guess." He was trying to be nice, but came off instead as slightly condescending. As if an enthusiastic response at one concert summed up an entire Canadian attitude.

"Where was that concert anyway?" he persisted. Jesus, did he really care? Just to appease him I came up with the first Canadian city that popped into my head:

"Ah, Regina. In Regina." An uncomprehending expression fell over Merv's face.

"Vagina," he whispered, incredulously, "you played in *Vagina*? You mean, there's a place in Canada called that?"

He looked at me as if he was going to cancel his show and fly right there on the spot. Tempted as I was to leave him with this heightened image of Canada, I dutifully spelled out *Regina* for him.

Merv was the first interviewer to nail down the angle of "Congratulations, you've got a hit in the States, so now you and your parents can come back and live here. Isn't America wonderful? Aren't you wonderful?" After that, the rest of the Stateside interviews followed suit. At the time, it reminded me of the simplemindedness of the Canadian media. Once they come up with an angle on you, it sticks. True or not, people are loathe to see through or work around it.

I was to find out later, however, that the US wasn't quite as inflexible as Canada when it came to a pop star's image. So many stars flood the media down there that the scrutiny of any individual star isn't as intense or rigid as in Canada. Here, the few stars we have are subject to microscopic scrutiny. The resulting image, although initially a boost to popularity, may eventually go on to overpower the performer. Hard as the performer tries to show growth or change, he is constantly cast back into the shadow of his old image. Eventually, the media begins to tire of this image and yet remains incapable of viewing the performer in any other way. Unless the performer has access to the American market, this usually marks the beginning of the end of his career. So many times when a reporter came to interview me, the accompanying photographer would ask me to pose with my shoes off. If I refused, there would frequently be an *illustration* of me with large, tearful puppydog eyes, bare feet, the works. So if a writer was actually convinced to do a balanced piece on me – one step forward – the accompanying illustration would simply drive the old image even deeper into the public's consciousness. Two steps back.

One of the problems here, unlike in the US or in Great Britain, is that Canadian performers need the media more than the media needs them. Although critics and radio stations can only survive by writing about or playing music, they can easily sell newspapers or keep ratings high by focussing on American or British artists. They can virtually ignore all Canadian artists except the ones who are already stars elsewhere. Those who put their trust in radio's Canadian content regulations are simply naive. Canadian radio, if it so chooses, can dump off its "Can-con" records in off-peak listener hours. Or they can play an American record that technically, if not culturally, qualifies as Canadian. For example, "Puppy Love" by the Osmonds is about as Canadian as George Bush; but because the song was written by Paul Anka, it qualifies as Canadian content. This isn't to say that Canadian musicians are necessarily ignored by the media here, but rather that the media can choose to ignore them without suffering serious consequences.

The initial stages of the American pop performer's career revolve almost exclusively around the hit single. A hit single immediately defuses an artist's dependancy on all forms of media except, of course, radio (video stations such as MTV or MuchMusic are really just a visual extension of Top 40 radio, so that if you have a hit single you're pretty well guaranteed heavy video exposure). American Top 40 radio is more scientific than judgmental about playing a record. If certain statistics or data bear out a record's likelihood of being a hit, they'll play it, personal taste notwithstanding.

Part of this is due to the "crossover" factor that plays such a major role in the US. There are so many different types of US National charts — from "R&B" to "Country" to "AOR" to "Adult Contemporary" — that a record can prove itself by rising to the top of these charts and then "crossover" onto Top 40 radio. In Canada, the crossover factor isn't as profound. This is especially difficult for our black performers. Canada has inherited much of America's covert embargo of black artists on Top 40 radio. Unless he's a superstar in the States, a black artist pretty well has to crack the Top 5 on the R&B charts before Top 40 will even give him a sideways glance. But, unlike the US, there's no R&B format here for a black artist to crossover from. Thus, the Billy Newton Davises and the Liberty Silvers languish in Canada; their only hope for even moderate success in this country is based on whether the American music machinery will eventually give them a shot Stateside.

Canadian radio stations follow the American charts very closely. They can afford to be cautious, watch a record develop across the border, and if it proves to be a hit then jump on it. No risk. The problem comes when a Canadian record is released only in Canada. Suddenly, they have to make up their own minds and usually they err on the side of

BLAST

JOEY GREGORASH

BACKGROUND:
Joey Gregorash was born in Winnipeg June 23, 1950. His first musical training came on the violin; but in his early teens he quickly switched to beating the drums with Winnipeg group The Mongrels. At 16, he became the band's lead singer, and, after hosting a Winnipeg dance party TV show, recorded his first single.

CLAIMS TO FAME:
He cut two albums in the early '70s, North Country Funk *and* Tell The People. *The first LP featured two memorable singles, "Jody" and "Down By The River", the latter written by fellow Canadian Neil Young. The single "My Love Sings" was released off the second album. The 45s were mildly successful in Canada, going Top 10 in some cities. Gregorash toured until the mid-'70s when he joined the creative department of Winnipeg radio station CKY where he won 15 writing awards. He later became a DJ.*

MUSICAL STYLE:
Good time rock-and-roll

WHERE IS HE NOW?
After trading the concert stage for radio, Gregorash joined CKY-TV in Winnipeg in September, 1986 as host of S'kiddle Bits, *a children's TV show. In May, 1987 he released the single "Together, The New Wedding Song", which hit #1 in many centres, and became a Canadian gold record. He is also touring again, doing a family-style show that includes tunes such as Elvis Presley's "Teddy Bear" for kids and "The New Wedding Song" for their parents.*

QUOTABLE QUOTE:
"It was tough to be on the road in the '70s. There was so much crossover, so many different kinds of acts out there. I packed it in when one guy (a club owner) if we had a trapeze act like the group before us. People were confused over what they really wanted".

FABULOUS FACT:
In 1988, Gregorash and partner Brian McMillan of Winnipeg wrote and produced the song "Golden Boy", a tune that focusses on Winnipeg boxer Donny Lalonde's fight against child abuse. With financial aid from the city of Winnipeg, the record, sung by Gregorash, also aimed to promote the city prior to Lalonde's November, 1988 bout in Las Vegas with American boxer Sugar Ray Leonard.

caution. That means playing a good Canadian record just enough to appear supportive, but never getting behind it with enough gusto to launch it (if it so deserves) into a bonafide hit single.

Without the power of a hit single, an artist's dependence on the general media increases. Music critics, video, TV appearances, even corporate endorsements — everything matters more. I would much rather play the hit single game, American-style than the media game in Canada. Getting on American radio is sometimes anything but pure luck, but once the song is on the radio its fate is decided by the public. And the record buying public is far more innocent, more *song-oriented,* than the media.

With the Canadian artist's increased dependency on all forms of media comes an uneasy intimacy of the two groups. Because of the smallness of the population and the fact that the music business is basically run out of just two cities (Toronto and Vancouver), everyone knows each other a little *too* well.

If ever there was a case of familiarity breeding contempt (or if you're lucky, mere indifference), it would be the Toronto media's attitude toward its musicians, particularly its better-known ones. I happen to believe that a person's talent is much more appreciated when you don't know the person. At times, the almost suffocating closeness of the media and performer fosters an undertone of competitiveness: when local journalist David Hayes interviewed me for an article in '81, he mentioned to me that at a certain time we had been "friends" with the same woman. He also stressed several times during the interviews that he too was a musician. Now to me that's just too close for comfort. Comparisons, conscious or otherwise, have got to creep into his perception of my talent. Please, give me Robert Hilburn of the L.A. *Times*. I'd rather entrust my fate to some hard-boiled, US Critic who didn't know me from Adam. In 1986, Liz Braun reviewed a Tammy Wynette concert for the *Toronto Sun*. In the review, she singled out Wynette's version of one of my songs: "That sloppy sentiment from Dan Hill called 'Sometimes When We Touch', but Wynette's treatment of the tune makes it sound stunningly beautiful. Some people would call that her immense talent. We call it a miracle."

My first real memory of Liz Braun is when she approached me after one of my sets in a small Toronto club back in 1975. Her enthusiasm for my music was boundless and although she always had a unsettling habit of castigating other Canadian singers as a way of building me up, she remained outwardly supportive of my music for several years. Now in fairness to Ms. Braun, she was my manager's secretary for a few years in the mid-'70s and went on to become publicist for CBS Records, where she helped schedule interviews for an album of mine in 1980. Obviously, your manager's secretary isn't going to denigrate you — at least to your face. But Braun led me to believe that she liked my music far more than any professional association she may have had with my career required. So, what happened when she became a critic for the *Toronto Sun*? Did this privileged appointment miraculously change her musical tastes? As a critic, does she feel pressured to maintain a certain image? I know one thing: If I lived in New York and Liz Braun didn't know me personally the only thing she would have mentioned about "Sometimes When We Touch" was that Wynette's treatment of it was "stunningly beautiful".

In 1976, another Toronto writer, critic and teacher, Bart Testa, wrote a pretty vicious review of my *Hold On* album for *Crawdaddy*, an American music magazine. The strange part was that Bart had written a very positive review for the same album just a few months earlier in a Toronto paper. Months before either review appeared, Bart made a point of getting to know me. He professed to be a great fan and even hung around backstage after several of my concerts, compliments abounding.

Of course, performers can be as dishonest as reviewers. I went through a period in my life where I didn't tell the truth to anybody – especially writers. This backfired badly once when Wilder Penfield of the *Toronto Sun* came to my home to interview me. In previous interviews with Wilder, I felt I had been too forthcoming about my personal life, and Wilder, as any good reporter should, chronicled my little mini-dramas a little too intimately for my comfort. So, at this particular meeting, I was determined to appear as ascetic as possible.

"My life is just too busy these days to find time for any social activity," I offered, rather lamely. Wilder nodded reverentially. He seemed to be buying it. Encouraged, I prattled on. "When I'm not writing songs or practising the piano – which usually takes about ten hours a day – I train for a marathon. You know, the usual stuff: 15 or so miles every morning".

At this point, Wilder looked like he was going to doze off from boredom. To spice things up a bit, I rolled up my pant leg and showed off my bulging calf muscle as some kind of tangible evidence. Once again Wilder nodded, this time more in self-defence than anything else, perhaps out of fear that I might decide to show him even more of my muscles. I was about to regale him with even more images of wholesome self-sacrifice when I heard a knock on my door. It was a teenage girl who lived in the neighbourhood.

"I'm just dropping off a package for you," she said sweetly, when I let her know I was busy.

"Just a friend of the family," I murmured to Wilder upon my return. I absent-mindedly opened the package as we listened to my latest record. Inside the package were three 8x10 black and white glossies of this girl, this 'friend of the family', quite naked. Tastefully naked – but still, naked is naked. Wilder's eyes damned near popped out of his head. He slyly made note of this in his article, writing something along the lines of "Girls from all over the city (they could be your daughter) make themselves available to his every whim and desire." Talk about conjecture – but still I got what I deserved. I suppose you're asking for trouble when you let a journalist interview you in your home.

But when it really gets dangerous is when a writer travels with you on the road. This happened to me in 1978 when I was touring the US with Art Garfunkel. The *Globe and Mail* sent Norm Snider to travel with me for several days. In a situation such as this, the first thing a writer tries to do with his subject is set up an atmosphere (read "illusion") of trust. Norm set this up early by letting me know how much flack he'd received by the *Globe*'s entertainment department for an earlier rather positive article he'd written on me. "They're very upset over how easy I was on you," he confided. "Critics, especially at the *Globe*, are very cliquey. If a writer's musical viewpoint doesn't fit in with theirs, he's ostracized."

Despite Norm's somewhat forced "us against them" chumminess, there was something odd about him. Whenever a female fan would come within 15 feet of me, he'd nudge me in the side. "Here's your chance," he'd coo. "Do you think she wants to sleep with you?" Alas, it became very clear that Norman had this fantasy of pop singers getting laid from coast to coast with a few concerts thrown in for appearance's sake. Although I was certainly no angel in the late '70s, I stayed clean during Norm's stay despite his almost constant egging on. Yet, in his article he so desperately tries to portray me according to his fantasy that even an innocent night alone gets written up as: "He's woken up enough times with a stewardess beside him talking about how she can't make supervisor that he's uninterested in repeating the experience." How does he know this? I certainly never made any mention of any past "stews" in my life. What Norman didn't mention in his *Globe and Mail* meets the *National Enquirer* exposé was that he was more intent on picking up women than just about any rock musician I'd ever toured with.

If a musician doesn't fit into the writer's preconceived notion, the writer often finds a way to make him fit in. The music journalist's job is to cut through the performer's image, and the attendant trappings of pretence and hyperbole, and deliver us on page as the real person. But all too often the writer falls victim to his own formula. The result is that the reader is no closer to the truth – the essence behind the singer – than if they'd be watching the most glossed-over video.

Larry LeBlanc's 1974 *Maclean's* piece on Anne Murray was a case in point. He seemed absolutely titillated by Anne's alleged lesbian following: "You know that guy who came on stage last night with the flowers?" she [Anne] said to the band. "It was a girl. I went to kiss him full on the lips, but just then he

BLAST

OCEAN

BACKGROUND:
Ocean formed in Agincourt, Ont. While still playing the high school dance circuit, it rose to the top of the charts worldwide in 1971 with catchy, religious-flavoured pop songs. The group's personnel changed through the years, but original members were Greg Brown, Janice Morgan, Jeff Jones, Dave Tamblyn, and Chuck Slater. With the exceptions of Brown, who lives in Oshawa, and Slater, who died a few years ago, the former Ocean members live in Toronto.

CLAIMS TO FAME:
Their biggest hit, "Put Your Hand in the Hand", written by Gene MacLellan, reached #2 in the US and #1 in Canada and other parts of the world. The band played throughout the world, scored chart success with "Deep Enough For Me", "One More Chance", and "We've Got A Dream".

MUSICAL STYLE:
Pop-rock with gospel influence

WHERE ARE THEY NOW?:
The group disbanded in 1975. After that, Brown got into the business side of the music industry managing a club. He is currently a financial planner, but plays music part-time around the Toronto and Oshawa areas. When his band plays more blues-style music, it's called Second Line Fever, but goes by the name Now and Then for other more pop-oriented gigs. Morgan sang with other bands, formed her own group Network, and came off the road in 1986. She worked as an excutive secretary at an insurance firm, but in 1988 became more fully involved with music again. Jones played for Ronnie Hawkins and with Red Rider, and now plucks his bass for singer Robbie Rae. Tamblyn is a carpenter/cabinet maker. Slater committed suicide.

QUOTABLE QUOTES:
Jones on Ocean's sudden fame: "No one was ready. Our idea with releasing this single 'Put Your Hand' was so that we could get our one-nighter price up at the high school circuit around Toronto. I'm serious, that's what we thought." Brown: "You sit down now 15 years later, and you think, jeez, you had a record that sold three million copies all over the world. If we had had the maturity to look at it in a different light, we could have used it as a hell o' a springboard."

FABULOUS FACT:
Ocean members were never too comfortable with their religious image despite the success of the songs. Contractual obligations proved frustrating to the band, and they earned little money for their fame and glory. Because of Ocean's situation, a law was later passed that prohibited artists from being signed unless their lawyers saw the contracts.

said something and instead I kissed him on the cheek. Then I noticed he had a smooth face just like mine." LeBlanc goes on to write: "She has the flinty good looks, the athletic figure, broad shoulders, and boyish hairstyle that naturally make her a darling of the butch set...Peggy Lee had a lesbian following. So did Janis Joplin. Why not Anne?"

Now it certainly wasn't wrong for LeBlanc to report this incident. What was wrong was LeBlanc's conclusion that due to a couple of isolated come-ons and her "flinty good looks" that she was a "darling of the butch set". I've toured with all sorts of female singers and seen all of them, from time to time, propositioned by other females. Surely LeBlanc isn't so naive as to believe that in the '70s this was a distinctly Anne Murray phenomenon. But LeBlanc had the perfect target: Canada's golden girl in career/image transition. There couldn't possibly be a better angle to fascinate the Canadian public than images of our own Annie: Lesbian fantasy object.

It all comes down to a calculated gamble for the performer. Do you chance letting a *Maclean's* magazine profile you? Obviously, the performer is using the exposure in the magazine as an opportunity to sell more records, while the magazine is using the performer to sell more magazines. It all depends on how badly you need the exposure. A performer of Anne Murray's stature, with access to heavy radio airplay all over the world, doesn't really need the magazine. The typical Canadian artist, however, will not have that massive radio support and will find it difficult to reject a magazine profile. *Maclean's* — Canada's so-called "national news magazine" — rarely runs a major story on a Canadian act unless it's already huge in the US. In 1978, David Livingstone contacted my management about doing a piece on me for *Maclean's*. Although I'd had two Canadian gold albums in '76 and '77, Canada's national news magazine showed no interest in me until I had a gold record in the States. When my manager told Livingstone we had to think about whether or not to grant an interview, Livingstone insisted that we make up our minds immediately. He wanted the article to run before "Sometimes When We Touch" peaked on the US Charts. I passed on the interview.

To my constant amusement, the reader rarely perceives an article the same way as the author or subject. I was barely 21 when a magazine piece was first written about me. I can remember the copy editor from *Toronto Life* phoning me for a "fact check" telling me how great the article was. To my surprise, I found the article to be quite snide. The writer called my songs "callow" and ridiculed my fans: "There's a flash of orthodontic braces, a glow of Clearsil . . . ".

"Don't worry," my father chuckled, "most people will read that you have a billboard on L.A.'s Sunset Strip and that you're being touted as the next Gordon Lightfoot. Be-

Our Anne, Mike Douglas and Jim Nabors: caught in the American hype machine

sides, no one knows what 'callow' means anyway." He was right. For weeks after that issue of *Toronto Life,* friends and media acquaintances alike phoned to congratulate me on the "terrific" article.

A successful pop singer or group has to understand the essence of his appeal and how that appeal applies to the infrastructures of the media. Doug Bennett (of Doug and the Slugs) may have more critical than radio appeal, whereas Bryan Adams' formula is the reverse. This isn't to say that an artist should give up on trying to win acceptance among media who thus far have reacted rather coolly — growth of any kind is critical to the survival of a pop artist.

But one should never be lulled into changing for the wrong reasons. My 1983 *Love in the Shadows* album received better critical reaction than any album I've made. Its detached production was the farthest thing from "typical" Dan Hill. There's something perverse about people liking you for not sounding like yourself. But that's what the Canadian media wanted and they got it. Yet the record sold poorly, and it was almost four years before I got another chance to make an album. During that time, I received all sorts of advice as to what kind of record I should make: "You'll never have a hit in Canada with a ballad," Polygram, my former Canadian record company warned me. The consensus in Canada was that I should avoid the soft stuff at all costs. The media and public wanted a rockier sound. But everywhere I went in the US, whether I was writing for other singers such as George Benson or Donna Summer or whether I was colaborating with other songwriters such as Michael Masser and Barry Mann, people wanted to hear my ballads.

Eventually, I ended up making another album that encompassed a variety of styles. The two hit singles were both ballads. Had I listened to the Canadian media and shied away from ballads I'd be out of a job right now. The US media, unlike Canada's, hadn't been overwhelmed by "the Dan Hill persona" (a persona the Canadian media played a huge role in creating). They were able to react to my songs more objectively. Here are the facts: "Can't We Try" failed to crack the Top 20. With a few exceptions, no one from the Canadian media was remotely interested in interviewing me until my record was already a hit in the US. I would've respected the media more had they stayed consistent and continued to be disinterested even after I'd come back to the US.

In Canada, the pop performer has to realize one thing: you rarely get any second

Doug and the Slugs: dismissed as a novelty act

Dan Hill: "Sometimes When We Touch" cemented his image forever

chances. Once your career has peaked, it's over for you in this country. Comebacks are almost unheard of. Not so in the US. Paul Simon, Billy Joel, Tina Turner; the list of stars that have returned after serious down periods is remarkable.

It's hard sometimes not to be bitter. It may be perfectly acceptable for the media to be condescending about your work, but if you respond in kind they're flabbergasted. Awhile back I did a CBC interview and the host expressed her disappointment that the singles off my album had been "only ballads". She went on to mention that she preferred two "rockers" on my album; yet I could tell that she hadn't really listened to the album. On the table beside her were a couple of reviews singling out the "rockers" as the most interesting songs.

"Could it be," she asked, "that Canadians had heard enough of your ballards after lyrics such as 'Sometimes when we touch the honesty's too much...'?"

Before I could consider a diplomatic response, I answered: "Listen, Canada is a nice place to live if you're not an artist; but, from a career standpoint, Canada only represents 5% of the world market share. So I don't waste a lot of time worrying about what Canada thinks of my ballads."

Well, this poor woman looked like she was going to lapse into apoplexy. "Oh no, surely you can't mean that," she scolded, as if giving me a chance to retract such a treasonous statement, "Canada must mean more to you than...than...that!"

Of course she was right, but damned if I was going to admit it to her at the time. Canada is my home and no matter how well I do elsewhere I'll always care too much about Canada's reaction to my music. I remember doing *Top of the Pops* in London, England, and hanging around backstage with Andy Gibb. This was 1978, the zenith of Gibb's career. Still, he was devastated by the negative media coverage he was receiving in his home country, Australia. At the time, I couldn't understand how it could get to him so; he lived in L.A. It was not as though Australia's backlash was directly confronting him. Now I understand.

Gibb's experiences with the Australian media touches on the question whether this bizarre relationship between performer and media is a peculiarly Canadian phenomenon. Courtship, honeymoon, career plateau, disenchantment, backlash, and finally being famous for once being famous: this supernova-style career happens more often than not to pop performers around the world. It's just that in Canada the process turns over more quickly. The media and the public desperately want to have their national stars. Indeed, the media plays a major role in creating them. But even more important for some reason is the need to tear down the stars we have. Once a Canadian performer's star begins to waver the media descend like vultures. It seemed as though every time I picked up a Toronto paper in '88, there was some mention of the disappointing sales of Bryan Adams' last album. The tone was almost gleeful. Naturally, no one mentioned that the sales of this "commercial disappointment" would still be in the top 1% of all pop albums released that year.

Although Clive Barnes' experiences with the Canadian performing arts are confined to the theatre, I had to laugh when I read his recent article in *Saturday Night* magazine. While living in London, England many years ago, Barnes was hired by that "formidable" Canadian critic and editor, Nathan Cohen, to contribute a weekly arts column to the *Toronto Star*. "...I collected items with a positively Canadian slant. But I soon discovered that what Nathan – or perhaps it was his top brass at the *Star* – liked even more than local-boy-makes-good was local-boy-makes-bad. I couldn't help but think that there was a certain national masochism here. Canadians...took more sour delight in some poor kid falling on his or her all-Canadian ass in full view of London than pride and pleasure in the Covent Garden triumphs of, say, Jon Vickers or Lynn Seymour... Nathan Cohen himself typified the hazy ambivalence a Canadian of culture and sophistication brings to Canadian art. He was so absolutely determined to be fair to Canada and Canadians that at times, without realizing it, he erred the other way. He applied rather higher standards to Canadian culture than he might have applied to artistic creations beyond Canada's borders."

A famous songwriter once told me that his father had always ridiculed his career. It became a major frustration in his life; it was almost an obsession to win his father's approval. He wrote dozens of international hits — pop anthems, in fact — but still his father remained cold and condescending. After his father died, he was sifting through some family mementos only to accidentally come across a huge file folder stored in the bottom of his father's dresser drawer. In the folder was a copy of every *Billboard* magazine chart that had included one of his songs. All the charts were filed chronologically over a ten-year period. Wherever one of his songs appeared, the title was underlined and his writer's credit circled. Obviously, the father cared much more deeply about his son's music than he cared to admit. Maybe it was a similar kind of duality of response that Clive Barnes was hinting at when recalling his experiences with Nathan Cohen. Perhaps the Canadian media cares about its artists much more than it realizes. Perhaps, as in the case of the songwriter's father, they simply have a difficult time expressing it. Certainly there is much more attention lavished on Canadian musicians than ever before. And maybe, just maybe, this has to be part of the reason why Canadians are starting to sell records in Canada.

Dan Hill first hit the charts a decade ago with "Sometimes When We Touch"; since then he has scored several hit albums and written hit songs for other performers.

8
COUNTRY & EASTERN

by Greg Quill

Rita McNeil: luminous imagery and powerful pipes

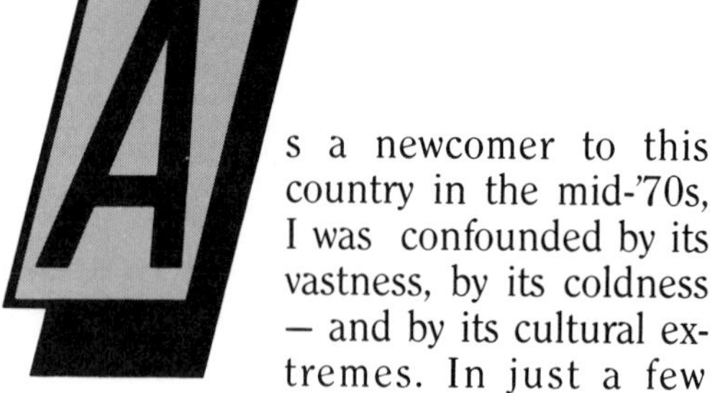

As a newcomer to this country in the mid-'70s, I was confounded by its vastness, by its coldness — and by its cultural extremes. In just a few months, I encountered people in Quebec who couldn't (or wouldn't) speak English and who preferred to endure my stilted, university Australian-Parisian rather than have me delight in their flexible, urban Franco-English. Or Anglo-French. Whatever. They were amused; I was glad I'd perservered with French. We made friends.

Still, the reality of a bilingual population was something for which all my dutiful study of things Canadian had not prepared me. Nor was I prepared for the mountains of ice and snow that hovered over black, frightened highways in northern Ontario's deep, sunless winter. Nor for freezing rain, which, in my first days here, caused me to slide some five industrial block-lengths up a steep incline on the Don Valley Parkway in my mate Tony's Peugeot — sideways, and at 90 km/h.

I wasn't prepared for Toronto's hard, civil facade, for its valuing acquisition and wealth over personality and talent, for its Puritan earnestness and, as far as I could tell, for its undeserved sense of self-importance. In fact, it seemed then that Toronto wasn't a hospitable place at all for adventures in the arts. It was disdainful, puffed up, bourgeois. It believed it had some kind of class when, in fact, it would not have even made the Top 50 of the most scintillating cities on the planet.

That Canada was as empty and terrifying as Australia, from whence I had embarked on my journey, didn't matter either. Australians in even the most remote corners of their country are curious about newcomers — friendly, generous, forgiving. That familiarity has always reduced the continent's actual dimensions. Luckily, Australians (Australians are always lucky) were novelties here in the '70s. They had a cute accent. They came from a sub-continent that might have

Stompin' Tom Connors: misunderstood and maligned ▶

been in another universe, instead of another hemisphere. They weren't British or European or American. They were different enough to amuse Toronto, and reasonably domesticated. And eventually, my mate Tony and I learned to make the most of our alienness. We made friends.

But yet, in the musical circles in which we plied our trade, we soon discovered that Canada's vastness didn't make just us strange to Toronto's arts and record industry barons. It also made French-speakers in Quebec exclusive, antagonistic, otherworldly; it made British Columbians "laid-back hippies"; and natives of the Atlantic provinces something worse, something less than civilized. "Newfie", we learned, was a generic insult with almost racist overtones that could be hurled as a weapon against anyone born east of Quebec's eastern border. Atlantic Canadians were, according to popular myth, poor, dull, under-educated, lazy, and culturally backward. They had less value than the Quebeçois,. who at least created Montreal and cooked fancy food. Maritimers drank to excess, ate saltwater fish, and "talked funny". Funnier even than the Quebeçois.

And their contribution to Canadian well-being amounted to a few "Paddy" songs, John Allan Cameron, Anne Murray, lobsters, and that peculiar delicacy, the fiddlehead.

Yet, in the musical circles in which we plied our trade, my mate Tony and I also discovered that Eastern Canadians were generally the most soulful, spiritually generous, straightforward, and honest of all performers. Moreover, they understood Tony and me better than all those disco-fied urban cowboy punks in Toronto. Easterners loved our music, which was built on British-and Irish-Australian folk forms, and they even carried on conversations with us without breaking into hysterics about our accents and colloquialisms – and without asking us to repeat every second phrase.

And suddenly it dawned on Tony and me that these people were just displaced; that their forebears lacked the proper criminal credentials, the wherewithal or the wisdom to cross the world, as ours had. Instead, theirs had just crossed the Atlantic. Maritimers were, nevertheless, *potential* Australians. They had guts. Somehow, a couple of hundred years ago, they'd simply gotten lost. Or maybe they were shipwrecked, en route, on Canada's inhospitable eastern coast.

It was a serviceable illusion, at least. And the notion was further reinforced when, some weeks after my first excursion as a rock 'n' roll bandleader into Canada's frozen wastes, Toronto's gritty, culturally observant little TV station, CITY-TV, aired – almost back-to-back, if my memory serves me well – director Don Shebib's 19th movie, *Goin' Down the Road*, and a music special featuring New Brunswick singer-songwriter Stompin' Tom Connors.

These movies were revelations to me. Their very existence confirmed everything I suspected about upwardly mobile, money-obsessed, and culturally constipated Toronto The Good: it was not the centre of Canada's creative universe after all. It was just the bank, the broker.

Goin' Down The Road, to my mind one of the best Canadian movies ever made, is a sad and wrenching chronicle of the crushing failure of two typically honest and naive "Newfies" who try to melt Toronto's cold, unyielding heart. The second movie, *This Is Stompin' Tom* (1972), depicts a contemporary version of what I've always imagined Woody Guthrie was to most of unsophisticated America in the '30s and '40s: a folk poet of uncommon conviction, an intuitive innocent who rendered the experiences and sentiments of the common man in the language of the common man, and who managed to relate simple, specific tales that were somehow universal in application.

Maybe it was the blood of my outlaw ancestors, maybe it was my own sense of alienation here, maybe it was the realization that these little cultural treasures had been withheld from the rest of the world as if they were an embarrassment, and maybe it was the echoes of Irish rebel ballads, of working songs and laments from my own past – but something began to draw me to the culture, to the music of Eastern Canada after I'd seen those movies. To the self-assured and wealthy of old Toronto, they confirmed a rampant axiom: Easterners are losers and rubes, permanent immigrants. To me, they represented noble battles for simple, human dignity against the forces of inherited money and bourgeois pretensions. And I've remained fascinated by that particular conflict ever since.

Most Canadians think of popular Maritimes music as vaguely country and western, remote, imitative, superficial. There's much to support the notion: Fiddler and country-swing band leader Don Messer, born in Fredericton, N.B. in 1909, was among the first Canadians to capitalize on the popularity of American country music with a Saint John radio show in 1929. Yodeller Wilf Carter, born in Port Hilford on the Nova Scotia shore in 1904, was the first Canadian to crack the popular American country music market with two songs, "My Swiss Moonlight Lullaby" and "The Capture of Albert Johnson", recorded for RCA Victor in Montreal in 1932. Hank Snow, born in Liverpool, N.S. in 1914, was a devotee of American country star Jimmie Rodgers and, with The Rainbow Ranch Boys, became a genuine Canadian country recording star in the late '30s and early '40s; he then settled in the US And became a staple of Nashville's *Grand Ole Opry*. And at the end of World War II new US-styled country performers emerged from both the Prairies and the Maritimes into the mainstream – Nova Scotia's The Bunkhouse Boys and Hillbilly Jewels (with Joe Brown, figurehead of 1970s country stars, The Family Brown) among them.

The impression that the Maritimes produces American-style country music still remains. Canadian country music star and multi-award winner Carroll Baker hails from Bridgewater, N.S. Anne Murray, from Springhill in the same province, has made every conceivable attempt to win over mainstream pop audiences in recent years and is without doubt Canada's most successful "crossover" recording star. Yet she is still classified and nominated for domestic and international awards as a country artist. New Brunswick-born Shirley Eikhard, the daughter of renowned Maritimes fiddler June Eikhard, has recorded several albums ranging in style from soft rock to mellow jazz since her first and self-titled folk-country effort in 1971, and still can't quite shake the "female country singer" Juno tags awarded her in '72 and '73.

But the popular music of the Maritime provinces is not intrinsically country and western, though the influence of the form, which first aired on US radio, was felt there before it was felt anywhere else in Canada, in the early '20s.

The chord, however, resonated through the Easterners' own folk memory, through Scottish and Irish ethnic traditions, through ancient narrative songs and ballads, through forms of communication and popular entertainment that were the first established in Canada. And they're still the strongest elements in a unique body of work, perhaps the purest and most resilient in our musical culture. We'll call it "Canadian Country and Eastern".

The best and most worthy artists in the field are those who have resisted — or who have simply not registered — the temptation to embrace American country music styles. It's a perfectly natural temptation, by the way; country music in the US sprang from simple folk streams and oral traditions that were in many ways similar to those of Canadians.

The US is a repackager and exporter of its cultural gifts. It pays little mind to imports. It's easy to understand why Canadians were easily seduced into imitation in those early years. Carter and Snow, mere entertainers in their time, followed the lead. And so did most western Canadian country acts; they still do.

But in the East, something else happened. A cultural imperative began to shape the music. Messer and his Islanders, already "old-time" music stars in Atlantic provincial dance halls and on local radio, became national favourites in the next decade, and regular network TV stars in the mid-'60s. Their music, comprised largely of traditional jigs, reels, and hornpipes — as well as Messer's own dance tunes — was not, he insisted, "Western or cowboy music…(but) hundreds

Don Messer's Jubilee: down-home music for the masses

of years old — folk tunes passed on from generation to generation."

It's true; in the best of Messer's work, recognized by folklorists and such fiddle archivists as Toronto's Graham Townshend as a synthesis of Canada's diverse traditions, you can hear the voices of history, particularly the history of the Eastern provinces. You can hear echoes of the songs of Omar Blodahl, born in 1923 in Saskatoon, but an adopted Newfoundlander who almost single-handedly collected, collated, published, and recorded a treasury of the province's traditional songs in the '50s and '60s. You can hear similar qualities in Newfoundlander Dick Nolan's repertoire, which embraced folk and country material from his home province and Labrador and was recorded on 11 albums (on the now-defunct Arc label) in the '60s. In the early '70s, after a series of national TV performances, Nolan even enjoyed considerable pop success with the traditional-style ballad "Aunt Martha's Sheep", then with other folk-based songs, "Home Again" and "Me and Brother Bill".

These were not country and western artists in any sense, though they were often portrayed as such on radio and TV shows. With Messer, a new strain began, one that would later feed into larger streams, carrying a taste of the Maritimes into pop, contemporary folk, rock 'n' roll — and into Quebec's already rich musical culture.

Canadian country and eastern doesn't travel well. For most of the past 60 years, the Maritimes and Newfoundland have supported and made regional stars of dozens of local singers and songwriters who will likely never make the cultural leap into the mainstream — to Toronto and beyond.

It's not the nature of the music that keeps these performers where they are; it's the unbreakable link between their own environment and the subject matter of their songs. Country and eastern is a functional music. It informs, narrates, spreads news and opinions, makes you dance, cry or laugh. But it's not lyrical in the purest sense. It's not art music; it was never meant to last. It's disposable once its job is done.

The work of the best-known Eastern Canadian country artists and songwriters — of Blondahl, Cape Breton's Charlie McKinnon, Connors, Nolan, Harry Hibbs, Roy Payne, Michael T. Wall, and Fortune Bay, Newfoundland's Simami duo — is drawn from specific local events and characters. Some songs, those dealing with, say, double-daylight saving time or off-shore territorial disputes between Newfoundland and French or American fishermen, don't have the same force outside the Maritimes.

Still, many have carried the styles and traditions west, only to find themselves representing the Maritimes and Newfoundland on TV and at folk festivals (as John Allan Cameron had done for more than a decade) or in the "Newfie" bars of every major city in the country. They remain prisoners to tradition, living souvenirs of "Down 'ome",

Carroll Baker: a down-home girl with a message ▶

or curious novelties for tourists and cultural philistines.

But a handful of performers adapted their skills as they went, forging songs that became tough and durable nuggets of truth and wisdom. Mind you, they were and still are generally misunderstood or misinterpreted by other Canadians. Connors, a prolific and gifted songwriter with some 1,000 rough, quirky pieces to his credit, became something of a cultural beacon in the early '70s, and was hailed by critics in national magazines and newspapers as a hero. For all that, Connors was never convinced city folk really liked him. Despite his success – he had released 29 albums by the end of the '70s, won countless sales and music-industry achievement awards, had been the subject of two movies, and had hosted his own series on CBC – he couldn't shake himself out of the conviction that he was a sort of sideshow freak. People only wanted to hear his hits, "Bud The Spud", "Sudbury Saturday Night", and "Big Joe Mufferaw", not the ones that he wrote last night or this morning. They wanted him to stomp a hole right through his trademark plywood board (on which, as a novice performer in Timmins, Ont., he had kept time for dancers in a hotel that had no amplification equipment.) And soon, of course, Toronto tired of him, turned on him, and discarded him.

Connors retired in the early '80s to a home in rural Ontario, and has steadfastly refused to perform, record or be interviewed ever since, despite pleas from fans, critics, and such media kingpins as CBC Radio's Peter Gzowski and Canadian cowpunk star k.d. lang. In late 1988, an album of new Connors songs was offered up most reluctantly – without the benefit of promotion or interviews. But it's difficult to find.

Payne was another country and eastern star whose considerable gifts were eventually spurned in the big city, but whose passionate "bleedin' songs" continue to burn. Born in Trout River, Newfoundland, he began writing songs in the army to amuse his friends, and, like Connors, wrote about working conditions, and the dreams and frustrations of ordinary people. But it was a joke song, "Goofy Newfie", and 500,000 sales of the album of the same name that earned Payne his first big break in the mid-'60s, with offers to record and work in Toronto.

He didn't adapt well. Booze first, then drugs claimed him, although he managed to record a handful of albums containing the most harrowing country songs, each a grainy map of a shredded spirit, for RCA and small independent labels in the '70s. Payne even worked as host of a TV series, *True North*, for Ontario's educational TV service, after he'd kicked his various habits, and was host of a live country music series for CBC-TV in 1974.

Still, he's seen as a victim, as one of those tragic characters in *Goin' Down The Road*; his legacy remains, his compositions actually define country and eastern music. But you don't hear much of Roy Payne any more.

And there aren't many performers these days who are carrying on where he left off. Cape Breton's Matt Minglewood, a hardy blues-rocker who can work an arena as if it was a tiny, crowded Atlantic coast bar, carries with him a wholesome share of Maritimes bravado. He has managed – over six albums (the best is '85's *Me And The Boys* on the Savannah label) and assorted forays into commercial rock in the late '70s and early '80s – to retain the character and flavour of the East, to write songs from the heart without fearing his roots will show, and to roam freely between traditional British folk forms, Atlantic blues (a tougher, more elemental style than the Chicago blueprint), and narrative country music that's occasionally breathtaking in its vulgarity and directness. There's not much poetry in Minglewood's music, but there's a whopping great heart and rivers of Celtic blood.

A similar strength, which stems from the inner assurance of an unassailable cultural identity, infuses the work of Edith Butler, a New Brunswick native, born in Paquetville. She prefers to be known as Acadian, as a member of that ancient and mysterious northern French-Maritimes community whose stoic independence forced thousands of them to flee political alliances during the War of 1812. They washed up in the bayous of Louisiana and hid there until late in the 19th century, when their music and lore began contributing to New Orleans jazz and evolving into what we now call Cajun, or Zydeco, music.

Butler performs mostly in French. Her songs are based on Acadian folk forms, which embrace simple, French-adapted jigs and reels perfectly suited to fiddle and accordion accompaniment. And she remains, if not the sole, then at least the most visible representative – in the national perspective – of her unique musical heritage. In recent years, Country and Eastern music has been more or less sealed away in Newfoundland, New Brunswick, Nova Scotia, and Prince Edward Island. In the late '70s and early '80s, Newfoundland's Wonderful Grand Band, a folk-based sextet that was led by Ontario songwriter Ron Hynes and often worked in concert with a set of satirists, who would later be known as the Codco troupe, made a valiant attempt at culture-fusion with the rest of Canada. They failed miserably and subsequently disappeared; what remains are the memory of two seasons when their WGB-TV series topped the ratings on regional CBC, and two extraordinary albums, a self-titled effort released in 1978, and 1981's *Living In A Fog*. Both received ecstatic reviews here, in the US, and in Europe, including Britain. Neither was ever distributed outside Newfoundland.

The one shining star in the country and eastern firmament in the late '80s is Cape Breton's Rita MacNeil, the 43-year-old mother of two grown children, whose sweeping, graceful country-folk ballads "She's Called Nova Scotia", "Flying On Your Own", "Reason To Believe", "Black Rock", "Two Steps From Broken", "Working Man", evoke not just the overwhelming presence of Atlantic Canada, but also a sense of its significance to the rest of the country. MacNeil, who worked fruitlessly in Toronto for most of the '70s as a singer and songwriter, supporting herself as a cleaner and window-washer, has never learned to play an instrument, yet composes songs of such grandeur and charm that she has become, in the late '80s, both wealthy and famous – across Canada and overseas. She possesses a voice capable of luminous, crystalline purity in the high register, and of a bluesy, gospel glow in the lower. And she possesses, more importantly, the memory of whence she came (Big Pond, outside Sydney; she lives there still), the memory of Scottish and Irish folksongs of her forefathers' tall tales, of the nobility of her working-class background, of the ruggedness of life, and of the richness of love. Rita MacNeil is Eastern Canada's revenge on snooty old Toronto; for she's the one who finally melted its heart.

She had some help: Ontario singer/songwriter Stan Rogers, whose ancestors were Atlantic Canadians and whose blood, he used to swear, was half salt water, spent his tragically short life re-inventing Maritimes folklore, or at least repolishing it – in the hope that it would glow as a proud beacon to other Canadians – in his own powerful songs. Though he stood squarely in the folk camp, many of Rogers' best songs – and most of those dealt with the Maritimes and Newfoundland of the 18th and 19th centuries – have passed into both the traditional oral and country music repertoires.

BLAST

KEN TOBIAS

BACKGROUND:
Ken Tobias was born and raised in Saint John, N.B. His early influences were Everly Brothers, and he began his singing career in the Maritimes on Singalong Jubilee. *He was also in the band Badd Cedes before going solo in the '60s.*

CLAIMS TO FAME:
Tobias' biggest hits were "Every Bit Of Love" and "I Just Want to Make Music". He also wrote the number one hit "Stay Awhile" for the Bells. His other solo hits included "Fly Me High", "Dream #2", and "Peace Of Mind". He's worked more behind the scenes in the past few years. Tobias has recently written film scores for European movies and Canadian documentaries, produced some of Corey Hart's early demos and has worked with other vocalists.

MUSICAL STYLE:
Ballads and upbeat soft-rock

WHERE IS HE NOW?:
Tobias lives in Toronto, writing songs, painting, and doing yoga. He worked on a children's album in recent years, besides his production and film score work; he still performs occasionally.

QUOTABLE QUOTE:
"I still can't believe how much they play my music [on the radio]. Right now, there are lots of songs out there that are sort of like what I would have written. They're in the rock bag, but they're mellower sorts of songs. But there are some bands out there that I'm totally against. Telling people that suicide is okay or that blackness is what's happening – I am totally opposed to that. I'm a warrior of light."

FABULOUS FACT:
Tobias was discovered by Bill Medley, one of the Righteous Brothers, who took him to Hollywood. While there, Tobias helped Paul Peterson of The Donna Reed Show *learn how to sing.*

Rogers achieved considerable fame in Canada and in the US with a handful of irreplaceable albums. He was a club and concert star, a big, burnished man who dominated every gathering at which he was present.

Yet he ached to be an Atlantic Canadian; he made himself out to be one, even as the region's cultural worth plummeted in the eyes of his peers. Rogers' poetry was never more vivid, his melodies never more stirring than when he sang of an imagined life in those provinces. Still in his mid-'30s, he died in 1983 in an airliner fire in Cincinnati, a grotesque twist of fate. He'd have preferred to die with a country and eastern ditty on his lips, battling a gale off the Newfoundland shoals. In the music of that place, may he rise again.

Greg Quill came to this country from Australia twenty years ago; after a long stint as pop critic for the Toronto Star, he is now the paper's television critic.

9

9 COMING UP TO FIVE O'CLOCK

by Terry David Mulligan

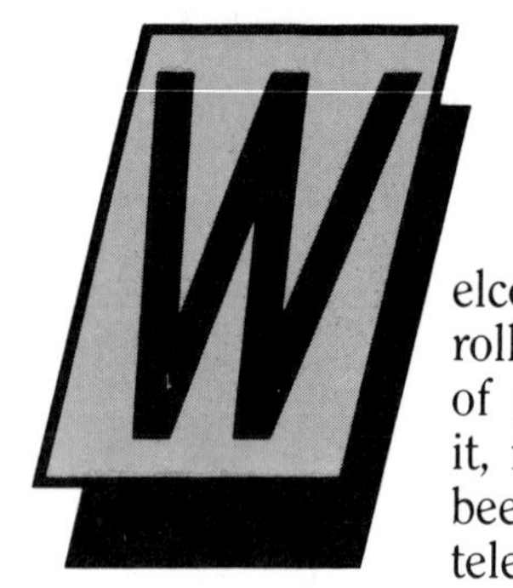

elcome to the weird, roller-coaster world of radio. Let's face it, radio has always been considered by television and print to be an annoying necessity. It's the ugly stepsister, or at least the lowest rung on the entertainment ladder.

There have been times when radio people actually believed this illusion. But the truth of the matter is that without radio there could be no music industry. Radio is the stage upon which rock 'n' roll has always played.

Rock is the metal, and radio is the magnet. That's the effect it had on me. Remember the scene in *American Graffiti* when Richard Dreyfus can't stand the thought of not seeing Suzanne Somers again, and finds himself at the local radio station because that's where the music and The Wolfman are drawing him like a magnet? In the movie, radio was magic; anything was possible.

That is exactly how I felt the summer of 1964. From the radio in the police car I was driving in Red Deer, Alberta, came The Stones, The Kinks, The Beatles, The Who, The Beach Boys, and Motown. It was one of the great years in all of rock 'n' roll. The person playing the music was one of the most sophisticated, coolest announcers I have ever heard. His name was Hal Weaver. He was blessed with a voice I would have killed for. He did his show standing up, snapping his fingers, always smoking, always on.

One day, I climbed the stairs to CDRD Red Deer, just as Dreyfus did in the movie. When I saw Hal Weaver work his special magic, I was hooked. As soon as he turned off the mike, he'd take the 45 that had just finished, throw it up in the air like a frisbee, and, when it dropped back down, he'd catch it, spin it on his middle finger and put it back in its jacket. He would repeat the same move in reverse with the next record and so on. Try doing that with CDs or tapes!

To the dismay of my parents and my peers, I left the security, prestige, and wages of the

BLAST

THE HAUNTED

BACKGROUND:
Best remembered as a raunchy underground band, The Haunted formed near Montreal in 1963 as Ventures-style instrumental band The Blue Jays, before evolving into the first version of the Haunted. An early lineup featured Jurgen Peter and Pierre Faubert on guitars, Bob Burgess on bass and vocals, Glen Holmes on bass, and Peter Symes on drums. Later, members included drummer Dave Wynne, singer Johnny Monk, bassist Mason Shea, and guitarists Gary Marcus and Al Birmingham. The group folded in 1970.

CLAIMS TO FAME:
The band's penchant for wild parties and outrageous stage antics once had it banned from playing in Ottawa. Band members used to throw their motel keys into the audience to initiate parties. Its first major break came in the mid-'60s when it won a Montreal battle of the bands, beating out Toronto's David Clayton Thomas and The Shays, among others. Its prize was a record contract, and its 45s included "1-2-5", a driving rock tune and probably its biggest hit; "Searching For My Baby", "Mona", "Out of Time". They also released a self-titled LP.

MUSICAL STYLE:
Driving Rolling Stones-style rock-and-roll

WHERE ARE THEY NOW?
Wynne works for Canada's trade department in Seoul, Korea. Burgess was music director and assistant program director at a Montreal radio station until 1986, and now works for a Montreal business publication. Birmingham and Peter both received their pilot's licences in the late '60s. Today, Birmingham runs a helicopter leasing company in Montreal; Peter lives in Richmond, B.C., and is an electronics technician with Canadian Airlines. Monk manages the theatre department at a Montreal restaurant. Burgess and Birmingham are writing songs and hope to form a new band with other former members of The Haunted.

QUOTABLE QUOTE:
Guitarist Al Birmingham on the band's wild stage shows: "For the time, I guess you could say we were raunchy. Band members used to crawl along the stage during concerts and bite our drummer's leg."

FABULOUS FACT:
A selection of The Haunted's material has been re-released in a two-album set, without the band's approval, and is popular in the US and Europe. Collectors say the original version of the band's LP, on the Trans-World label, is worth $150.

RCMP for starvation, alienation, and the thrill of rock 'n' roll radio. In my quest, I moved to Calgary, Regina, and then back to my home town, Vancouver. And along the way I had the honour of helping to program Canada's first underground FM station, CKLG-FM (now CFOX).

If you were working in radio in Canada during the '60s, '70s or '80s, there was only one mission in mind: to become so good that you were hired by CHUM in Toronto. If they employed you, you had achieved the highest status possible.

Nevertheless, over on the West Coast, we had our own heroes, both human and corporate. The biggest and the best was Red Robinson, Vancouver's first rock DJ. His effect on the late '50s and '60s was huge. He was succeeded by one of the most admired yet unpredictable announcers ever: Fred Latrimouille, known as Latrimo. Vancouver also boasted one of the bizarrest broadcasters of all: Captain Midnight (J.B. Shane), who still lives in Kitsilano. Of the stations, Vancouver's CFUN was once the pre-eminent rocker on the coast until CKLG took over in 1968 in a shake-up of the market.

Edmonton had the mighty rocker CJCA, then CHED. Calgary had CFAC. Windsor took pride in CDLW, a powerful station that at one time was #1 in 14 US States. Regina had a Mutt-and-Jeff routine going on between little CJME and giant CKCK. Winnipeg was a great radio market in the '60s and '70s with such celebrities as Doc Steen, Daryl Burlingham, Dino Corrie, Boyd Kozak, Mark Parr, Chuck Dann, plus its rock 'n' roll war between CKY and CKRO. They also had a fantastic local rock scene to work with.

In the East, there was CHOM and CHEZ/CFGM and CFCF, in fact too many to single out. But if we look at CHUM-AM and FM alone, I think a complete picture of the growth of Canadian rock radio can be formed.

CHUM-AM hit the air in 1945, but the story doesn't really start until Alan Waters purchased it on December 11, 1954. On May 27, 1957, CHUM went Top 40, and at that time introduced their famous CHUM chart. Almost immediately, CKEY went Top 40 as well, and the race was on for Toronto's airwaves. The two stations waged a war through the late '50s and early '60s, and it was CHUM that came out on top more often than not. CHUM-AM maintained that top position against all comers (such as CFTR) until they themselves left Top 40 in 1985.

Radio is known for its characters – the announcers who are still fondly remembered today by four generations of listeners, some of whom now run the country. (Scary thought, eh?) CHUM'S first star was the happy Hungarian, Al Boliska, who was the morning man from the mid-'50s to 1963. He was replaced by Jay Nelson, once a kids' show host at WKBW in Buffalo. Jay ruled Toronto morning from 1963 to 1981. For almost 25 years, they were the only two morning men. They were surrounded by personalities for the other airtimes: John Spragg, Pete Nordheimer, Mike Darrow, Dave Johnson, Bob Lane, Bob Macadory, and Gary Ferrier.

ROBBIE LANE AND THE DISCIPLES

BACKGROUND:
Toronto-based band Robbie Lane and the Disciples formed in the mid-'60s, and flourished in clubs and on television throughout most of the decade. The band, with some new members, is still performing today, mostly in the Toronto area. The members are Robbie Lane (vocals), Torry Bush (guitar), "Wicked" William Cudmore (harmonica and sax), Doug Copeland (drums), Gene Track (bass), Paul Mifsud (tenor sax), and Bill Davis (keyboards). Davis replaced Paul Denyef in the past year. Lane and the Disciples all live in and around the Toronto area.

CLAIMS TO FAME:
The band's hits included "Fannie Mae" and "Ain't Love a Funny Thing". They backed up Ronnie Hawkins in the '60s, and were the host band of the 1960s national TV show It's Happening.

MUSICAL STYLE:
Rock-and-roll, rhythm and blues

WHERE ARE THEY NOW?:
Robbie Lane and the Disciples reunited in the mid 1980s and played clubs throughout Canada. Lane has always stayed in show business as a manager and an entertainment consultant. In 1988, he was host of a live version of Wheel of Fortune *at the Canadian National Exhibition. He hit it off with Vanna White and was asked to audition as a replacement for former host Pat Sajak. Lane made it to the final four but didn't get the job. However, White's manager is now representing Lane in Los Angeles should any game show jobs become available. As for the other members, Bush played in various bands after the Disciples, and is a commercial and jingle producer. (He wrote and produced the "I Adore My 64" jingle for Commodore computers.) Cudmore works for a business machines company; Copeland works for Bell Canada; Track is a chiropractor; Mifsud works with computers; and Davis is in the pharmaceutical business.*

QUOTABLE QUOTE:
Lane: "You can't just throw a band together and go out on a nostalgia binge and expect people to accept it. People, especially the younger generation, are far more critical today, and they have every reason to be."

FABULOUS FACT:
Although the band is best known for their TV work on It's Happening, *Lane says it pushed them toward more "bubblegum music", the kind of music they definitely* don't *play these days. Also, Bush sang the theme song for* The Littlest Hobo *TV show.*

Darrow, Spragg, Macadory, and Ferrier would go out to various charities as a singing group known as the Chummingbirds. (Name me four DJ's who'd do that today!) Ferrier put his radio looniness to work as a writer for TV's WKRP. Larry Solway brought open-line programming to Toronto with his *Speak Your Mind* show. All these guys were legendary, not only to Toronto audiences, but to jocks all across Canada. We wanted to be where they were.

CHUM created their own legend. CHUM was Toronto. They not only brought The Dick Clark Caravan to Toronto, they brought Dick Clark himself. They presented The Beatles in 1963. And CHUM was fun in the '60s. On April 1st of one year, they switched announcers with CKGM in Montreal, both DJs in both cities carrying on as though nothing was wrong. Pierre Berton, for God's sake, used to do a daily commentary for CHUM. That's where his broadcasting career first started. He even had his own jingle.

I think some people seem to forget the tough road AM radio had to run. In the '50s, it just wasn't taken seriously; then along came TV and knocked radio on its collective butt. What saved the medium were stations such as CHUM. Realizing that TV had booted radio out of the living room, CHUM adapted and started to show up in the kitchen, the bedroom, the car, and on the beach. The station saw a new role for radio in Canada: personable, portable, and keyed to *now*. Not only did these changes at CHUM spread to other stations and other markets in the '60s, they're still being felt today. For many many years in Toronto, if there was something important, something somehow historical in a rock frame, then CHUM was at the centre of it, was in effect creating it by becoming part of the story. Being a vital part of Toronto, CHUM-AM and FM became the predominant rocker in the Canadian market since 1957, a truly remarkable achievement.

Is today's CHUM as much fun as yesterday? I don't think so, certainly not for the announcers. Today, we're dealing with positioning in the marketplace, controls, machines instead of people. Jocks back in the '60s and '70s would drive the program director crazy because he couldn't be following us all seven days a week. So we'd take advantage of this freedom, and we were forever short-circuiting the system. You can't do that today. As a result, radio is dull, predictable, boring as hell. Only the good stations will stand out now, meaning the ones willing to ride the edge — the stations with general managers and executives who remember what free-form, creatively structured radio was all about. Today, stations proudly announce ten to twelve record sweeps. What the hell is that? Why bother? Put on a damn tape and forget about radio. The Jock has become a button pusher, nothing more. It's all tighter, briefer, shorter, duller.

As much as I loved spinning great three-minute hits on AM radio, I think I really found my medium when I switched to FM, which is the real mover of music hits in today's market. For the longest time, J. Robert Wood and the consultants around him at CHUM-AM in the '60s resolutely refused to acknowledge the FM side down the hall. CHUM-FM received its licence in the fall of 1961, and played classical music for the first seven years.

Only in 1968 did CHUM adopt a progressive FM format, much like CKLG-FM in Vancouver and the great KSAN in San Francisco. It was on Canada Day weekend in 1968 when CHUM-FM brought Murray The K in from New York to kick off the new format. CHUM-AM became the only North American station to take its AM call letters and successfully transfer that heritage to its FM side.

Even Murray The K couldn't have imagined what was to come. Every fruit loop, nut case, AM reject, and draft dodger headed for jobs on progressive FM. But as always, it was the good ones that rose to the top. Those were wild times, friends. The music was killer stuff, the mix was anything you could get your hands on.

Then in Montreal, CHOM-FM and CKGM-FM both started heading to progressive. CKGM was headed by a guy named Norm Winer (who would later program WBCN Boston), and was owned by a true radio flake, Jeff Sterling, who at times wore a black robe and nothing else. The first experiment at CHOM just didn't work: it was too far off the edge. In came Dave Marsden, Earl Jive, Doug Pringle and, from the States, Mr. Warmth (Don Shafer), and suddenly CHOM FM had good reason to believe it was programming some of the best progressive FM in North America. They were great years at CHOM FM. Even today, stories abound about how crazy the CHOM jocks were in the late '60s, how it was without a doubt the craziest station ever to hit the airwaves. Bob Lane, General Manager at CHUM-FM, thought so, which is why he stole Shafer, Jive, and some of the best of CHOM's team. But though CHUM hired CHOM's on-air staff, they never had the guts to just let them go. There were always those controls so typical of CHUM.

CHUM-FM in the early '70s was Pete and Geets in the morning slot, along with the wonderful Larry Wilson in the newsroom, Shafer on middays, Chuck Azzarella on afternoons, Marsden in the evening. Jim Bower did late evenings and David Prichard went all-night. This line-up through the '60s had tried its damnedest to stay free-form and free thinking; but their nemesis was the format-crazed AM program director J. Robert Wood, who for all his brilliance as one of foremost programmers in the business, never did grasp what FM radio was all about. Rick Ringer replaced Shafer, Rick Moranis replaced Azzarella, who moved on to start the wonderful CHEZ-FM in Ottawa, Pete and Geets went to CFNY, and John Donabie moved to the Coast and back.

The late '60s and early '70s were a wonderful time to be an announcer. The jocks on CHUM-AM/FM could (and did) make and break records, not only in Ontario but in other stations as well, because we all watched what they did and would more than likely play their chosen records. If you were a group and CHUM didn't play you, the road to the top was that much tougher to travel.

The turning point for CHUM-FM was in 1977, when it was decided to format the station and make it a major factor in the Toronto market. At the same time, Q107 came into being and stated its "kick-ass" rock 'n' roll years. CHUM-FM went from being one of the first and best progressive FMs to a highly commercial — and successful — FM giant.

My question about radio has always been: Is it fun for the audience? Does it make them talk about you? Can you move them? Do they care about you? To a man, if you ask the people who were on the inside during the '60s and '70s, they will tell you that radio did all of that during those years, but very few do it today, including CHUM-FM. Today, the CRTC regulations have pushed programmers toward the safe centre, and do not encourage stations to take risks or to experiment. Audiences during the '60s, especially for CHOM, CKLG, and CHUM-FM, were involved, they were part of the station, they weren't numbers on a graph.

CHUM-FM is admittedly #1 in Canada's most competitive market today because the forces at CHUM decided that a mainstream CHUM-FM was their best resource for the future. It was a corporate decision made, not on the streets, but in a boardroom. That's what's happened to radio in the '80s. Many of the guys in those suits listened to CHUM-FM in the '60s and '70s, but have rejected true radio values in favour of corporate gains. In my heart, I realize I'm holding on to an ideal, a vision of radio that's rare today. But in my head, I know these stations are doing whatever they have to make a profit, and I can't blame them for that. Occasionally, I find little pockets of what used to be; stations that run on the edge, with announcers that create weirdness just beyond the twilight zone. And, irony of ironies, one of the gems still out there turns out to be MuchMusic, a video network whose audio signal is on cable FM throughout the country, and is, without the pictures, a great radio station. Led by the free-thinking Moses Znaimer and John Martin, MuchMusic still allows its on-air staff to be individuals, and challenges them to create and communicate. CHUM-AM and FM can no longer make or break a record, but MuchMusic can and does offer the only opportunity for new groups to get day-to-day national exposure no matter where they live in Canada.

MuchMusic is owned by CHUM Ltd., which now owns twenty-five AM/FM stations across Canada, and is the world's largest private broadcaster, with holdings at CHUM/City-TV, ATV Television, TV stations throughout the Atlantic provinces, Music Plus in Quebec, and of course the jewel in the TV crown, MuchMusic West, home of yours truly. Much's profits for the fiscal year 1988, less agency commissions, was $159-million. At least with MuchMusic they are continuing the tradition of radio for the people that was established by CHOM and CHUM in the '60s; so, all power to them.

Terry David Mulligan, the original host of CBC's Good Rockin' Tonight now hosts MuchWest on the MuchMusic network.

10
THE BIZ

by Richard Flohil

Paul Anka: have chutzpah, will travel

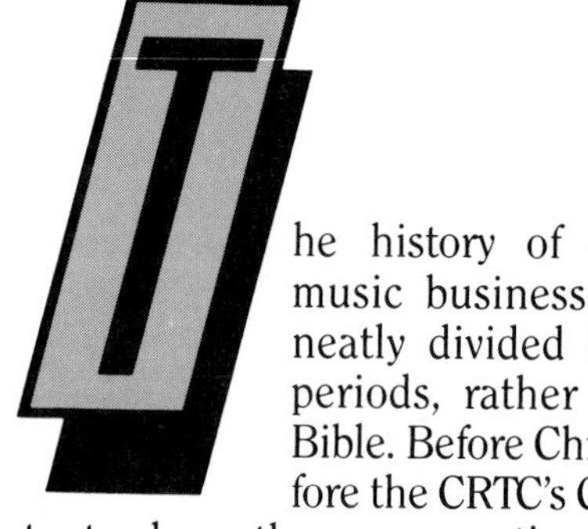

The history of Canada's music business may be neatly divided into two periods, rather like the Bible. Before Christ – before the CRTC's Canadian Content rules – there was a nation of unbelievers. After the CRTC, there was a viable music industry, viable, if only marginally efficient. The Canadian music industry is still overloaded with problems and doubts, sometimes confused and often confusing, and it is run by some of the nicest people in the world. It is, then, very Canadian: polite, gentle, considerate, hesitant to say no, and usually grey around the edges. Attempting to view it in perspective, let alone in an historical perspective, is like looking in through a kaleidescope with a smudged lens.

In the distant past, before 1960, Canada had accidental hit artists such as the Four Lads, the Crew Cuts and the Diamonds, who did what American stars such as Pat Boone did – ripped off black music and sold it, like white bread, to the multitudes. Their citizenship was incidental and they scored their hits in the United States; Canadians were pleased for them. Moe Koffman had a massive instrumental hit and at about the same time, Paul Anka finally talked his way into an American record deal and delivered a smash hit "Diana", first time out.

The business people were in New York, and the first of many familiar warnings passed into legend: Go south, young man, if you want to break into the music business. In Canada, there simply wasn't a music business, just a tiny group of would-be agents, would-be managers, and would-be bands on the way to New York or California – if only they could get a visa, a lead from a friend or relative, and an old hearse to make the trip in.

Canada didn't even get a music trade paper until the early '60s, and the founder of the first, a charming Brit named Ray Sonin, a former editor of the British music paper, went broke in the land of opportunity in less than six months.* He was succeeded by an

The Guess Who: wheatfield soul from the Prairies

ex-RCMP constable, Walt Grealis, who struck up an unlikely partnership with small-time record producer Stan Klees who needed a medium to promote his label, Red Leaf Records. The magazine Grealis founded, a flimsy amateur broadsheet called *RPM*, still limps on, 25 years later, although its influence has waned and most people read it only for a remarkably bitchy gossip column (still called "Walt Says") contributed by its founder.

But in the mid-'60s, there was beginning to be stuff for *RPM* to print press releases about. Ronnie Hawkins, all bullshit and moonshine whiskey, had arrived from Arkansas and recruited a band that later became known as The Band; The Guess Who were making their first records; CBC television was airing Singalong Jubilee out of Halifax with a freckle-faced singer called Anne Murray. And on Toronto's Yorkville Avenue, hippies crowded the Riverboat and the Penny Farthing and the Mousehole, and singer-songwriters were everywhere, trying to express themselves just like that scruffy kid in New York, Bob Dylan.

The fact was that there was little demand for Canadian bands, precious little radio play for the handful who did make dismally-produced 45-rpm records, and no infrastructure to support any groups that managed to emerge from their parents' basements. There were some modestly successful only on a regional basis. Mandala, the Lords of London, and The Shays (with their lead singer, David Clayton Thomas) were stars in Toronto, but couldn't get arrested for causing a disturbance in Winnipeg (or even Ottawa). The Esquires, a big deal in Ottawa, were nonentities in Toronto. J.B. and The Playboys were a Montreal-only phenomenon; The Collectors were a big deal in Vancouver, but only won real acceptance outside their local area when they changed some members and their name and emerged as Chilliwack.

The business scene, however, could be most charitably described as dismal. Neil Young had left for Los Angeles; Joni Anderson had married a sadly untalented Detroit folk singer called Chuck Mitchell, and disappeared; Gordon Lightfoot and Ian and Sylvia and a band called the Paupers were all managed by a portly New York wheeler-dealer named Albert Grossman. The big names on the business scene were Bernie Finklestein, who managed his artists (a loud band called Kensington Market, and later folkies Bruce Cockburn and Murray McLauchlan) from a telephone booth outside the variety store on Yorkville Avenue, and a dapper young man called Mel Shaw, who managed a cleancut band called The Stampeders.

The amateurs who were on the scene were just that — amateurs. They ran little clubs, booked the local bands as best they could, and tried to figure ways to get to New York. This writer, in a move typical of the times, was convinced that Murray McLauchlan would never earn a penny, and passed on the chance to manage him. A few months

The Band: *an all-American sound from Kitchener, Ont.*

The Stampeders: cowboy harmonies

earlier, he had sat in a Yorkville coffee house, muttering doubtfully as a portly young man called Paul Hoffert outlined his plans to create a "really hip" big band to be called Lighthouse. Like all the others on the edges of "the scene" (yes, that's what we called it), he loved the music, but couldn't possibly see the slightest way of making any money at it. Small-time agents hung around seedy offices over coffee houses, and fans became "managers".

Flash forward to 1970. A time for action. We are losing our "stars". There are too many broken dreams — in a business where broken dreams are the stuff that successes are built on. But pop music is a cultural industry. Money will accrue to Canada if Canadians can get hits abroad. The government would like to help. It is now time to talk about the CRTC rules.

The case for the Canadian Content regulations is watertight. If Canadian music is played on Canadian radio, the performance royalties collected by both CAPAC and BMI Canada, now PROCAN, will be earned by Canadian songwriters, rather than being sent to members of affiliated organizations outside the country (ASCAP and BMI in the United States, PRS in Britain, and SACEM in France, among similar organizations around the world). If Canadian bands are to be recorded, it will be necessary to build studios to record them in. And if Canadian records get played on the radio, Canadians will want to hear Canadian bands in person, and they will have a chance to play for people outside their immediate hometowns. The demand for Canadian record companies will be created to market the records. Pierre Juneau, who headed the CRTC at the time, was an heroic visionary — really — and he became the first patron saint of the music industry, and that's why we named our Juno Awards after him.

Canada's radio industry had been warned,

April Wine: jacks of all trades – ballads to anthems

Kim Mitchell: suburban realism

loud and clear, that legislation was on the way. Alan Waters at the CHUM group did what he could to forestall the inevitable by forming something called the Maple Leaf System, in which major stations across the country (including all the CHUM stations, of course) agreed which Canadian records they would play, so that some kind of consensus of hit status could be arrived at. For the first time, hit records on a national basis began to emerge.

The effort to forestall the Canadian Content regulations failed: in January 1971, the CRTC rules became reality. Mention of the CanCon rules still produces – all these years later – glazed looks, exasperated sighs, and mutters of discontent on all sides. At the close of 1988, the president of one Canadian record company angrily wondered out loud why he was part of a delegation going to Ottawa to demand that FM radio stations meet a 30 percent Canadian Content standard (the figure set for AM stations). Too often, he pointed out, Canadian radio stations met their CanCon requirements at 10 at night or early on Sunday mornings in special programs colloqually known in the radio business as "Beaver hours"; Canadian records were not programmed at peak drive-time listening hours; and the 30 percent requirement for AM radio was seen as a maximum to be reached, and never as a minimum to be exceeded.

This is no time to go over the regulations in detail once again (as Louis Armstrong reputedly said about jazz, if you have to ask you'll never understand). They did not, however, meet with the approval of the Canadian radio business, which opposed them vigorously on several grounds. Philosophically, this was government interference in private enterprise; practically, it was impossible to play so many dreadfully produced records. Alternatively, there were not enough Canadian records to play in the first place.

Triumph: light shows and fast licks

Loverboy: struttin' sexism

Listeners would hate the Canadian content programming and defect, wholesale, to American border radio stations. And the rules would place an intolerably burdensome record-keeping task on Canadian stations ill-equipped to handle it.

In the first flush of optimism, dozens of new recording studios did open, independent record labels proliferated, new releases cluttered radio music directors' offices, and some of the major American companies in Canada made more-than-reasonable commitments to Canadian artists. Alas, some of the studios went broke in the next five years, many of the artists – recorded too soon in the bloom of optimism – were never heard of again, and too many music directors had smug told-you-so expressions on their faces as they threw the majority of the new records in the garbage as simply unplayable.

However, the results soon began to look a lot better. Some of the best of the new studios survived and prospered (Manta in Toronto, Le Studio in the countryside north of Montreal, and Little Mountain Sound in Vancouver). The two performing rights organizations were able, as they had promised, to dramatically increase their payments to Canadian composers (from some $600,000 in 1969 to well over $3,000,000 in 1976). Soon, however, they began to notice another fact: the income coming from abroad for Canadian songwriters was also increasing (from $200,000 in 1969 to $1,300,000 five years later), which indicated that Canadian music was getting dramatically more popular outside Canada. **Agents in Toronto who, pre-CRTC, had been able to book a tiny handful of bands outside of Ontario, were soon able to place bands across the country; one agent reported that by 1975 he'd been able to book no less than 50 bands from Ontario on coast-to-coast tours.

The list of artists who achieved national (and, in a handful of cases, international) recognition in the early '70s began to lengthen dramatically. The key singer-songwriters who had attempted to get their careers into gear in the '60s began to find success. Neil Young, Joni Mitchell, Gordon Lightfoot, Ian and Sylvia Tyson, Leonard Cohen, Bruce Cockburn, and Murray McLauchlan are all active today, to some degree or other. In fact, Canada's pre-eminence in this genre probably stemmed as much from the fact that singer-songwriters were easier and cheaper to record than bands as from the fact that we're sometimes an introspective lot, given to contemplating our psyches and having lacklustre love affairs.

But the bands were doing fine, too. Canadian content holdovers from the '60s included The Guess Who and Lighthouse and Blood Sweat and Tears, whose material was mostly written by their singer, a beefy Toronto rounder with a juvenile prison record called David Clayton Thomas. As their stars waned, Bachman Turner Overdrive, Rush, April Wine, Dr. Music, Crowbar, Triumph, and dozens of others began to make an impact. And suddenly a whole range of middle-of-the-road acts moved into prominence, including Anne Murray, now 20 years after her debut, an international superstar and still one of the best singers anywhere. In the '80s, with Canadian radio play guaranteed and a growing infrastructure in place, dozens of more acts came (and in some cases went) with varying degrees of success: Max Webster, The Box, Men Without Hats, Toronto, Loverboy, Platinum Blonde, Gowan, Rough Trade, Martha & the Muffins, The Spoons, Kim Mitchell, and Bryan Adams among them.

A catalogue of Canadian artists is one thing; a look at the business structure is another. The most important organizations in Canadian music, of course, are the international record companies. There are seven of them – in descending order of size, WEA, CBS, BMG (formerly RCA), PolyGram, Capitol-EMI, MCA, and A&M. Between them, these organizations (all but PolyGram with their Canadian head offices in Toronto), distribute the labels owned and licensed by their parents – but, most importantly for our purposes, close to 40 smaller, mostly Canadian-owned, independent labels. In addition, some of the multi-nationals – most notably WEA, Capitol, CBS, and BMG – were, as the '80s grew to a close, signing a variety of Canadian artists to international recording deals. This was sometimes a mixed blessing, because simply signing a deal in Canada no more gurarانteed success in the United States or Britain than it did in Canada. Some acts (just ask the guys in Platinum Blonde or Kim Mitchell or Gowan) did spectacularly well at home, but failed miserably in the United States.

The growth of independent labels in the late '70s and throughout the '80s was encouraging. In some cases, the labels were owned by successful rock bands and their management people (Aquarius was founded on the fortunes of April Wine; Anthem on the massive success of Rush); in other cases by enthusiastic fans who learned their job by trial and error (Holger Petersen's Stony Plain label out of Edmonton, or the industrial music people who run the Nettwerk label in Vancouver). Sometimes Indie labels stuck with particular genres of music, but the largest of them, Attic Records, built a catalogue that included the Rovers and Anvil, The Nylons and Hagood Hardy, Haywire and Lee Aaron, Killer Dwarfs and Teenage Head, not to mention dozens of foreign artists that owner Al Mair and his staff discovered at

Platinum Blonde: from Police covers to teen idols

MIDEM, the annual music industry trade fair in the south of France. These signings, usually licensing deals for individual albums and/or singles, ranged from George Thorogood to the Chieftains and from Jennifer Warnes to Motorhead.

Many of the independent labels, however, found the business tough going. Almost all of them were (and remain) under-capitalized. Some went spectacularly broke, including the unfortunately named Solid Gold label. Others were (and are) essentially vanity labels designed to showcase an individual act, and usually one unable to get a deal with a larger Indie, or one of the major multinationals. Collectively, however, the independents acquired considerable clout by forming CIRPA (the Canadian Independent Record Production Association), which certainly outgunned CRIA, the association formed by the multinational labels, when it came to grabbing the ear of government.

In Ottawa, the mindset that had helped create the CRTC regulations was encouraged by the activity that was being generated. By the early '70s, Pierre Trudeau was photographed wearing Crowbar's souvenir necklace, which was not only decorative but made a handy tool for nasally ingesting illegal substances. Pop music may not be art, the mandarins conceded, but it was a cultural industry. While the Canada Council kept its nose out of the rock 'n' roll business, all sorts of other government entities tripped over themselves in the following years to offer encouragement, support, and money.

This culminated, in the mid-'80s, with the creation of the Sound Recording Development Plan, under which the Federal Department of Communications promised to give the recording industry $5 million a year for five years. In English Canada, these funds were administered by FACTOR (the Foundation to Assist Canadian Talent on Record), yet another organization best known by its initials. By 1988, the total was exhausted six months into the fiscal year, and the Canadian independents who benefitted from the largesse (and 40 percent of it was assigned to support the Quebec music industry, desperately hampered by the small size of its marketplace) took to pointing out that $5 million a year was a pittance, compared to the benefits available to the film industry, and went cap in hand for more.

The growth of a recording industry infrastructure – good studios, major label activity, and a relatively healthy independent recording picture – was being matched by other developments. The Juno Awards, started by *RPM* magazine as a social gathering in 1971 (Stan Klees' mother made the sandwiches) were glitzed up into a major CBC television show and taken over by the hastily concocted Canadian Academy of Recording Arts and Sciences. A new trade magazine, *The Record*, began in 1981, and provided a

***Rush**: months on the road at the time*

The Nylons: accapela wonders

dramatically improved internal news service for the industry, which, as the '70s were concluding, was relying more and more on Billboard, the major American trade publication, for news and radio programming information.

In fact, Canadian media has – since the late '60s – been amazingly supportive of domestic pop music; even the *Globe and Mail* covers the pop scene these days, even though the publisher is privately convinced that rock 'n' roll is the major cause of the decline of Western civilization. The early "underground" magazines have come and gone (only Vancouver's *Georgia Strait* still exists), and in Toronto the advent of *Now* magazine has had a remarkably uplifting effect. Better still, its ad rates are so inexpensive (compared to the dailies) that every promoter in town uses the paper to hype their acts.

The most important new player in the media mix has been MuchMusic, which has singlehandedly given an amazingly wide range of pop acts national television exposure. And in addition to the exposure, Much financially supports VideoFACT, which distributes monies to make new videos – a requirement forced on it by the CRTC, but nonetheless a welcome source of income for independent bands with more creative energy than cashflow.

In 1988, important changes were made to the Copyright Act, and these, too, are certain to have a dramatic effect on the business climate. There are few topics in the music business that induce boredom as rapidly as copyright, but the changes to a piece of legislation that had remained virtually unaltered since 1926 have been important. For instance, the 1926 Act specified that composers would earn 2 cents per song per record sold; that "statutory rate" was abolished, and it is likely that composers (when the dust has settled) will now earn close to 6

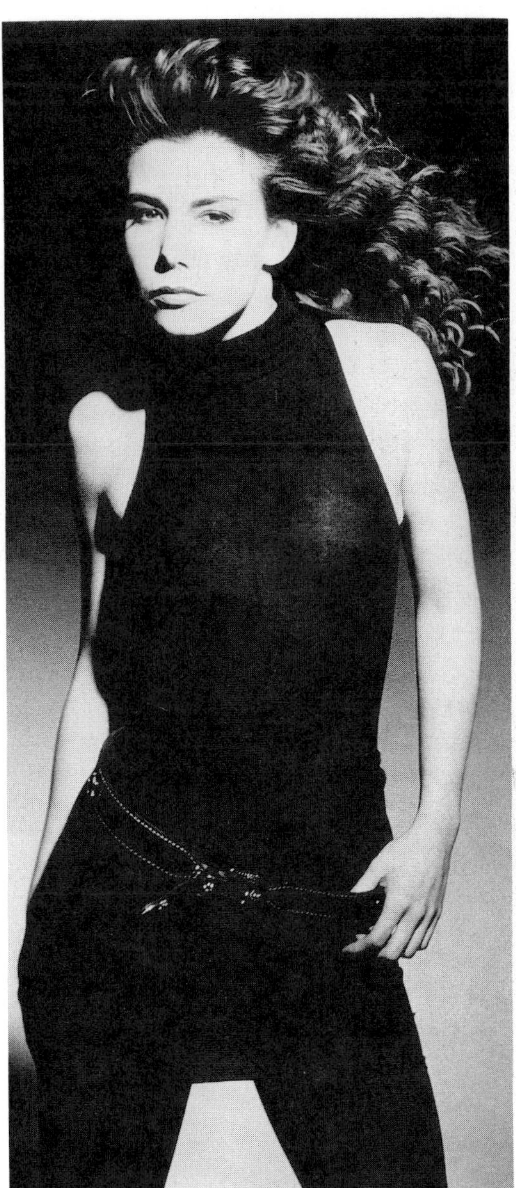

Lee Aaron: the metal queen of the headbanger set

Bryan Adams: stripped-down rock 'n' roll for the kids

cents. Penalties for piracy have been drastically increased (the previous penalties for forging records and tapes were a mere slap on the wrist, and were rarely invoked in any case). And coming up in a second round of changes to the Copyright Act may well be a levy on blank tape to recompense record companies and artists for the massive "home" duplication of pre-recorded music.

But the mainspring of any business are the people who run it, and the music industry in Canada is effectively run by about 300 people, including the managers, promoters, club owners, record company brass, key media people, heads of major retail chains, and the people who run the various industry asssociations. With hardly any exceptions, these people are remarkably nice, upstanding, straightforward, and — a blessing for new people trying to get into the business — remarkably accessible.

They are also moral. Of course, favours are exchanged, backs are scratched, and hands wash each other; this is a very small business, and everyone knows everyone else. But payola is almost unheard of, and the people whose job it is to promote records and hype new music do so without distributing money, cocaine, and sexual favours to radio program directors. This is a fact of life north of the border, which astonishes visiting Americans.

The biggest weakness in the industry is a lack of a distinct class of entrepreneurial managers. Any artist's manager is only as good as his act's last hit; but there are too few people like Bruce Allen (the prickly, funny, hard-nosed, pussycat collector of Coca Cola memorabilia who manages Bryan Adams and who believes that pop music begins and ends in Vancouver) or Leonard Rambeau, (the soft-spoken Maritimer who has run Anne Murray's consistent career for well over 20 years). Music business management is an art learned on the job, and managers

The Jeff Healey Band: *down-and-dirty blues from a clean-cut kid*

need money, patience, promotional abilities, basic business and babysitting skills, some legal knowledge, and above all, credibility and a phone book full of numbers and contacts. They also need to be hardnosed.

Somehow, we seem to be just too nice to breed this sort of person. Artists' managers in Canada hardly ever say no, even when they need to; they certainly lack the go-for-the-throat ability that has kept Bruce Allen in business for years, starting out with Bachman-Turner Overdrive. The tiny few who do shout at people, bully their agents, bluster their acts into position, and lean hard on the record company people who sell their product, are universally known as "difficult" and/or "temperamental" and are not trusted. And the manager, of course, will earn all the blame if something nasty happens to the act, or if nothing happens to the act.

The other side of that, of course, is that the Canadian music industry really is a nice place to be. Canadians have learned how to make "American" records (often using a mix of government money and investment capital), and every now and then we can proudly check favourite names in Billboard charts as an indicator of how well we're doing. After all, our track record is okay, at least until you compare it with the Australians who work from a smaller market base. And the Australians, to their credit, have been successful in selling songs about Australia to North Americans, something we've been unable to do since The Guess Who did an album called *Wheatfield Soul*, which also included an embarassing song about Gordon Lightfoot (that most "Canadian" of artists to earn international success).

But new Canadian artists can get record deals in Canada – and if they can't get deals, they can make their own records, and hope a "real" independent company or one of the multi-nationals will pick up the ball. If the music is in the grooves, as they used to say before the advent of cassettes and the CD, they can get airplay on Canadian radio, they can sell records nationally, and they can travel by van from Newfoundland to Victoria Island playing clubs and concerts. American acts, in places such as Minneapolis, or Dayton Ohio, or Austin Texas, find it much harder to escape from their own immediate geographical surroundings.

What's the future? Probably more of the same, plus occasional surprise success stories (similar to that of k.d. lang) and steady, straightforward progress. We'll continue to create stars – thankfully more often by accident rather than by design – and they'll continue to yearn for the American market. And, despite the question marks raised by the lowering of trade barriers (jeez, will the big American companies move, leaving no-one here to distribute our Canadian records),

Frankie Venom of Teenage Head: a party-hearty favorite

Colin James and Keith Richard: a rising star with big-time friends

we'll continue to cope. We'll continue to take government help, and continue to feel guilty about our dependence, as well as complaining that they didn't give us enough money. Our radio stations will still grouse about the CRTC rules, and the CRTC will maintain the status quo.

And we'll still make good music, and we'll still be able to discover and nurture brilliant artists who may not "make it" on the charts, but will strike chords in the hearts, minds, and feet of their listeners. So what else d'ya want anyway? This is Canada, eh, and we're getting by the best way we know how. We're not getting rich, but now – unlike in the distant days – we're at least getting work.

Richard Flohil, long-time manager, promoter and gadfly, is now director of Toronto's Mariposa Folk Festival.

**Sonin later became a very successful disc jockey in Toronto with a nostalgia radio show on CFRB called* Calling All Britons. *The show is still on the air in 1988, although Sonin is now in his seventies.*

***The 1987 performing rights income from abroad for Canadian composers is now close to $6,000,000, almost as much as the amount they earn from domestic radio and television airplay.*

11
IN THE BEGINNING, THE WORD

Bruce Cockburn: lyricist with a conscience

by Wilder Penfield III with Bernie Finkelstein

nce upon a time there was a fusion of literate lyrics and musical music. Gilbert & Sullivan; Rodgers & Hammerstein; Lerner & Loew; Cole Porter; George Gershwin; Harold Arleh, and so on.

In Canada, well, there was Gene Lees…

Tin Pan Alley remained relatively kind to the wordsmith. But rock 'n' roll wasn't. "Everybody's Doin' The Loco-Motion" was rather more important for momentum than for momentous lyrics. In Canada, there was Paul Anka, who got away, and Andy Kim, who got "Sugar Sugar" to the Archies, and Ronnie Hawkins, who got here with 40 Days… Canada was still resting on its roots in a branch-plant slumber.

Then came the folk revolution of the '60s. Suddenly the word was king. And Canadians, who knew from folk, temporarily took over the world. Songwriters don't come more regal than Joni Mitchell or Leonard Cohen or Gordon Lightfoot or Buffy Ste. Marie or Ian and Sylvia or Neil Young.

Soon, rock incorporated folk, and became aware of its own importance. For a remarkable time, rock lyrics were actually being rated for honesty and lyricists for integrity. Newspapers began to hire token young persons such as me to spread the words. Maybe they wanted us to build bridges across the Generation Gap, which no longer exists, but seemed like a big deal at the time. The music that defined Us threatened Them. But the lyrics were mined for meaning, quoted by politicians, taught in school.

Bernie Finkelstein was managing rock 'n' roll bands, including the Paupers and Kensington Market, for whom he actually wrote some lyrics. He was amazed that Lightfoot lived in Toronto:

"Gordon Lightfoot's lyrics happened to say more to Canadians about Canadians than all previous movies, plays, and books put together. Therein lay the creation of a Canadian identity. And suddenly it mattered to the world.

"My experience comes from inside the

Murray McLauchlan: a roadhouse folkie ▶

Ian Thomas: the songwriter as sex symbol

music business. You might even call it myopic. But not since the Group of Seven had any group had such impact on this country. But unlike the Group of Seven, who are perhaps only now beginning to gain some recognition outside our borders, this group was immediately recognized.

"In the '60s, Americans knew precisely three things about Canada. There was a lot of snow, though not as much as they thought. There was lots of hockey, which we soon sold out. And there were lots of great singer-songwriters. (And if we'd known how to sell that out, we would've.)"

That was the Golden Age of Canadian Lyrics. If your American cousins can quote more than the "hook" from the lyrics to a Canadian song, chances are it's from a musician who was formed in the '60s:

"The best of them derived their lyrics for the whole of our environment. First of all it was the landscape — lakes and trees, "Four Strong Winds", "Helpless", "Canadian Railroad Trilogy", "Now That The Buffalo's Gone", "Acadian Driftwood", "Goin' To The Country". But soon our environment was recognized as more than high winds, white sky; it was "16 Lanes of Highway", it was "Down By The Henry Moore", it was "American Woman", it was love from both sides and touching her perfect body with her mind. Gordon Lightfoot singing "You can't jump a jet plane/ Like you can a freight train" said more about change in two lines than any social historian might in a whole thesis. And the words our songwriters used to define our world became the music that defined us."

A second wave of great Canadian lyricists, hot on the heels of the first, was dominated by songwriters that Finkelstein managed — Bruce Cockburn, Murray McLauchlan, Dan Hill:

"Among other things, Cockburn had helped re-invent the singer as landscape artist —

BLAST

A STITCH IN TYME

BACKGROUND:
A Stitch In Tyme formed in northwest Nova Scotia in the '60s when two local bands, The Untouchables and The Continentals, joined forces. After some success in their home province, the band moved to Toronto where it became a part of the Yorkville music scene. A Stitch In Tyme members were Bruce Wheaton, Grant Fullerton, Bob Murphy, Donny Morris, and Pinky Dauvin.

CLAIMS TO FAME:
The band was known for its strong vocals, and made it onto the charts in 1967, a rarity for Canadian groups in those pre-Canadian content days, with a cover version of The Beatles "Got To Get You Into My Life". They were regular fixtures in Yorkville and played at Expo 67.

MUSICAL STYLE:
English pop emphasizing strong vocals

WHERE ARE THEY NOW?:
After Stitch broke up, Wheaton formed Everyday People and later the east coast band, Molly Oliver. He lives in Nova Scotia and performs solo in east coast clubs and bars. He has a studio in his basement, and wrote a song in 1987 for charity. Fullerton played in Lighthouse and still performs in and around Toronto as a solo act, and also with a three-piece rock and blues group. He lives in Stouffville, Ont. and has been the host of a blues show on Toronto radio station Q-107. He also performs annually in the Caribbean. Murphy was in the country band Big Buffalo, and now lives on a farm in Nova Scotia. Morris has performed with Wheaton in the past and does solo work. Dauvin, who also was in Lighthouse, lives in Toronto. They have played annual reunion gigs for the past three years.

QUOTABLE QUOTES:
Fullerton on the group's vocal style: "We'd dissect every part of a song until we got it right. It was a source of pride among us. We had five vocalists and we used them." Wheaton: "It was great, unreal. It was incredible for a band to have that much popularity. I think it would have been a matter of time for the band to make it really big if we'd stuck together... but ego trips got in the way."

FABULOUS FACT:
A Stitch In Tyme was different from many of the musicians in Yorkville at the time. Most bands were either into rock, rhythm and blues or folk. A Stitch In Tyme gained enormous popularity by concentrating on doing cover versions of English groups of vocal harmony bands such as The Beach Boys and The Four Seasons. They broke up shortly after trying to switch to doing more original material.

that was one of his metaphors. But by the mid-'70s, all three were defining what the world had in common with Canadians and what Canadians had in common with the world.

"Lightfoot and the Tysons got us to the railroad stations, to the airports; McLauchlan took us right downtown. He was in Kensington Market on the first album jacket, and he was stains on a sink inside."

But his biggest hit was "Farmer's Song".

"Even this was written as the salute of a city kid. And it foreshadowed what he did on that CBC series called *Heroes*, and on the album of the same name."

Dan Hill was at another extreme. He was a romantic; his word-pictures were internal.

"Dan explored the whole passion of love, with all its nuances. "You Make Me Want To Be"..."Sometimes When We Touch"... People got down on him for being so sensitive; it embarrassed them – especially, in that era, coming from a guy. But he was concerned with what was universal. And the experiences that inspired his lyrics were very personal, very specific, his expression may be uniquely Canadian in its openness."

Other Canadians came up with individual songs that were as fine as any we've mentioned. Bernie cites David Wiffen's "Driving Wheel", Willie P. Bennett's "White Lines", Stan Rogers "Peggy's Cove".

"Meanwhile rock and lyrics were getting divorced on the grounds of disco. Remember disco? Well, it's still here, and words are still getting electrobeaten to death. However, for better or for worse, the creation and endless repetition of phrase fragments has never been a Canadian forte.

"Nor was punk, the rough reaction to the slick insistence of fashionable dance music. Canadian cities did spawn some decent punk bands, but nothing memorably indecent, nor much in which the deliberately irritating form was fuelled by genuinely provocative content.

"Canuks mostly maintained the middle road. Our biggest successes were in commercial rock. Four lyricists came to the forefront: Burton Cummings, Randy Bachman, Jim Vallance (with Bryan Adams), and Gino of the Vanneli Bros. You may not find their rhymes in poetry anthologies, but you can clearly hear their music when you see their best-known phrases: "Stand tall", "You ain't seen nothin' yet", "Straight from the heart", "I just wanna stop", and so on.

Likewise Loverboy ("Everybody's working for the weekend") and Eddie Schwartz ("Hit me with your best shot") and April Wine ("Rock 'n' roll is a vicious game", which is as close to good advice as I could give). I just

Tommy Hunter and Ian Tyson: urban cowboys

wish the music business wouldn't spend so much of its time copying what has just happened. No wonder the baby boom audience apparently wants to take its heroes with them. Those heroes wanted to make a difference. The commercial stars want to make the same difference.

"Chilliwack asked itself some hard questions. Triumph came up with some memorable anthems. The idea of a collective such as the Perth Country Conspiracy was revived by other collectives, such as the Parachute Club and Harmonium and Kate & Anna McGarrigle.

"But the biggest exception to the commercial-rock rule of the '70s was Rush. The Toronto trio may have been the last of the great purveyors of old-fashioned progressive rock, but they also have one of its more inventive lyricists in drummer Neil Peart."

And now it seems that we're entering a time when people are treating lyrics as something important. Once again. It's probably too early to predict lasting importance for Tom Cochrane, Rita MacNeil, Mary Margaret O'Hara, Andrew Cash, maybe even for performance artist Anne Siberry. But Carole Pope has already had an influence on our sexual politics. And the purer tradition — our singer-songwriter specialty — continues to evolve in the work of performers such as Connie Kaldor and Ferron.

"Ann Mortifee and Diane Dufresne took that tradition into the realms of sophisticated theatre. Valdy took folk back to the roots he shares with other coastal creators such as Gene MacLellan and Stompin' Tom Connors. The tradition of the lyricist who sang what he had to say continues to develop in different directions, but it has never died. And at times it has been the strongest element in the public expression of our culture."

I have a theory about why it became so important here: Evolution in Canada, where the distances between paying gigs were so great, dictated that the survivors were those who could practise their craft often — solo, mobile, flexible, affordable performers. Also, the horizon Canadians saw for themselves was virtually endless, rich with possibility and foreboding — perfect fodder for songwriting.

That has changed. The distance between Toronto and Winnipeg is just the same in 1989 as it was in 1969, but it sure seems different.

"Cockburn has gone as far away as Tokyo, Kathmandu, and Santiago to nourish his

BLAST

MOTHERLODE

BACKGROUND:
The members of Motherlode, Steve Kennedy, Wayne Stone, Kenny Marco, and William Smith, first got together as players in Grant Smith and the Power. When they decided to go out on their own, they moved to London, Ont., Stone's hometown. They had almost no money and slept on friends' floors. They made their debut at London's Image Club. On releasing their first single, they skyrocketed to fame.

CLAIMS TO FAME:
Their only hit was "When I Die", written by Smith and Kennedy; but in 1969, it climbed to #18 on the influential Billboard chart and also hit the Top 10 in Canada. However, shortly after the song peaked, the group broke up because of management problems.

MUSICAL STYLE:
Soft rock

WHERE ARE THEY NOW?:
Kennedy, Stone, and Marco all played in the influential jazz-gospel-rock band Dr. Music after their Motherlode days. In fact, Kennedy wrote one of that band's most successful songs, "Sun Goes By". His life in music after that was a rollercoaster, and he admits that drinking problems were one cause. He gave up drinking and playing several years ago, and has worked operating a collating machine at Commercial Lithograph Inc. He continued to study music throughout. However, in the past year, Kennedy has returned to music playing with a local Toronto band. Stone also cut down his playing because of a muscle ailment. However, he studied music at Humber College in Toronto in the 1980s and is currently teaching there part-time. Marco plays music in Saskatchewan, while Smith is a top session player in Los Angeles.

QUOTABLE QUOTES:
Kennedy, on the band's only hit, for which he wrote the lyrics: "When I Die" was about the difficulty of being a musician, and the struggle, and your family putting you down because they think you're a bum."

Stone, on his memories of Motherlode: "It was an experience of a lifetime, really, and you keep trying to reach that same height. Once you've had that degree of energy you experience with that kind of success, life is never quite the same. But it's not a bad feeling. It's a good feeling because you've had it and most people haven't."

FABULOUS FACT:
"When I Die" didn't receive any Canadian airplay when it was first released. Only when it started climbing American charts on the west coast did DJs here follow suit.

sense of adventure. Neil Peart too. They still seek the challenge of different perspectives."

Nonetheless, Cockburn always works from a Canadian base. It's easy for people to miss the fact that even the Third-World songs always had a Canadian context. And now we have U2 quoting Cockburn back to the world in the live *Rattle & Hum* album.

But I still wonder why, when the world decided it was time for word-workers such as Tracey Chapman and Michelle Shocked and Bruce Hornsby and Billy Bragg, why we weren't competing in the same arena, which was traditionally our greatest strength. Other branches of Canadian entertainment are dominated by "cultural industries". Music rides on its stars. But if you've been living here since '64 and don't agree that lyrics represent the best of Canadian culture… well, take of, eh?

Wilder Penfield III is former rock critic and is now the current book critic at the Toronto Sun.

Bernie Finkelstein is Canada's manager par excellence; the artists he represents include the likes of Bruce Cockburn and Murray McLaughlan.

12
VIZ A VIZ VIDEO

by John Martin

Leonard Cohen: comeback fueled by innovative video

The Most Important 16 Videos in Canadian Pop

Blue Rodeo, "Try": When Blue Rodeo put their first album out in 1987, it sat there for six weeks. It wasn't picked up by radio. Nobody cared whether it lived or died. Then they produced a video for "Try". We loved it at MuchMusic. We added it in major rotation, they then were added at every radio station and the album went gold. The rest is history and it wasn't me doing that; it's the band doing that, and management doing that and the record company doing that.

The video was a really nice piece. But sometimes it's a question of distribution — just being there — rather than something unique inside the video. It's a great song, it's a great video; it works. So you can actually measure the impact of video with something like that.

Leonard Cohen, "I Am a Hotel": "I Am A Hotel" was — and is — one of the few attempts to marry the concepts of music video, the images of music video and the pace of music video in a television show. So instead of a television show being designed as a television show, it was designed as a series of music videos, each of which told a story — and when linked together, they formed a full experience, if you like, as a series of chapters in a book. It was also important in the sense that it was designed to prove to people that you didn't have to be a head-banging, leather and lace, heavy-metal-person to use the genre. That there was an opportunity to use the skills and crafts to do something a little elevated — a marketing tool that could also be art. It demonstrated that people such as Ann Ditchburn and Leonard and everybody else had taken the form seriously. And

Glass Tiger: the new internationalists

it brought together a lot of the people, over the course of its manufacture, that went on to become important to the video industry.

Janis Joplin, "Peace Train" Somebody recognized the fact that when Janis and friends travelled cross-country by train in the '60s, there would be unique film footage available – not just of the concerts – but on the train and the interaction between the artists on the train. There were jam sessions on the train – interaction that was quite unique. But they ran out of money when they were making the film. People hid the film because they weren't getting paid. Eventually somebody found some of them hidden in people's refrigerators with the ASA markings ripped off. The only cohesive footage that he could get rights to was the Joplin material. And he made this feature film based on that material. It shows Janis Joplin in the kind of situation that we weren't used to in those days – Janis among her peers, reacting like a normal human being and being a musician with her peers. She drank, she threw things, she was a warm person – she was all of everything that we have now learned to appreciate about her. But here it was on film and that was unique. Nobody was shooting those films then. You saw Elvis in the Ed Sullivan show but you didn't see Elvis at home. That was one of the first examples of what television could do with a rock 'n' roll artist using the power of the media.

k.d. lang, "Crying": k.d. lang is one of the great success stories in recent Canadian memory – much of which can be ascribed to her use of video. She and her manager, Larry Wanagas, recognized early on that the way to get her across the country was to use the vehicles that were available – video. Because of the geography of this country, it is nearly impossible to take a regional artist and tour her with any hope of success – or any hope of financial success, certainly. So instead they made a very inexpensive video. And they used the news media to get the message out. On the basis of that, people who were booking clubs in Toronto and the east coast of Canada knew what to expect and booked them with enough regularity that they could tour the country. Then they made a more sophisticated video and did the same thing again – instead of going to radio – because they had a problem that she was such a mixed artist. Nobody knew whether she was a country singer or a rock 'n' roll phenomenon or Elvis Costello in drag. But television didn't make the same distinctions as radio.

When she went into the United States, instead of becoming another radio phenomenon, the traditional route of country music, she did the Johnny Carson show. They went into the studio and they did a video of her with all the old country greats – which immediately made her one of them to the audience's perception. All smart moves – and one of the more brilliant moves, the more poignant moves – was "Crying", which she did on the late Roy Orbison. It's fabulous – two people with amazingly wonderful chops. The soundtrack is just extraordinary and gorgeous, but the video too is nicely underplayed. First, there's the mystery image of Roy Orbison that we've all loved: the man in black with the shades. And floating behind him is this mystery woman with the most amazing pipes in the world. You just float through the video – it's a gorgeous piece.

Rush, "Closer to the Heart": I don't know how important video was early on to Rush. They're the kind of people who are forward-thinking so they would have been aware of it. Yet I don't think that you can ascribe any of Rush's success to video. Instead, they stayed on the road three hundred days a

BLAST

JON AND LEE AND THE CHECKMATES

BACKGROUND:
The Checkmates, reputed to be one of the hottest soul bands in Ontario, formed in Toronto in the early '60s with lead singer Lee Jackson (a.k.a. Michael Ferry), Michael Fonfara on keyboards, bassist Dave McDevitt, guitarists Larry Leishman and Al Dorsey, and a drummer, whose name no one remembers. It became Jon and Lee and the Checkmates in 1964, with Jackson and John (a.k.a. Jon) Finley on vocals, Leishman on guitar, Peter Hodgson on bass and Jeff Cutler on drums.

CLAIMS TO FAME:
Most of its gigs were in Ontario high schools and teen clubs; but the group also opened twice for the Rolling Stones at Maple Leaf Gardens in 1964-65, and played for 65,000 people at the opening of Toronto's new city hall. The Checkmates tasted limited fame in New York in 1965-66, working at the Phone Booth where the Young Rascals often performed, and at Shea Stadium with Junior Walker and the All-Stars, the Chiffons, and the Temptations. In 1967, it released its only record, "Bring It Down Front", a soul ballad went Top 10 in Toronto. They recorded a second song, "Girl, Beautiful Girl", that was never released. The members were growing in different directions and the band split soon after.

MUSICAL STYLE:
Funky, intense soul

WHERE ARE THEY NOW?
Finley played with a number of bands before moving to Los Angeles where he's a soloist for a black gospel choir. He wrote "I Will Serenade You", a big hit for US Pop band Three Dog Night; Jackson worked at the Toronto Stock Exchange and ran a small recording studio before joining a floor covering firm 15 years ago; Fonfara played with various acts, including the Electric Flag, Foreigner, and Lou Reed and the Lincolns. Today, he runs a recording studio. Hodgson played with Rough Trade; he now works in real estate in Toronto. Leishman works for Motorola Canada Ltd. in Mississauga, and Cutler is a movie producer and set director.

QUOTABLE QUOTE:
A typical Checkmates show would see Finley spilling his personal miseries onstage with his emotional brand of gospel-style vocals while co-lead singer Jackson had the fans moving with his energetic dancing. Even the godfather of soul James Brown was impressed. Finley remembers the wild crowd reaction the band could elicit: "We'd get screaming, heaving emotional reaction from our female audiences. We played London Ont. one time and we needed bodyguards. The women would go nuts."

FABULOUS FACT:
After the Checkmates, Fonfara and Finley played with the innovative US band Rhinoceros, and were joined later by Hodgson and Leishman. The Los Angeles based group had a memorable hit in 1969 with the perky instrumental Apricot Brandy.

year for the last fifteen years. And that is — and was — their strength. Today, it seems extraordinary: no bands do that. They only did it because that's the way that they do things.

But because Rush are really extraordinarily forward-thinking people, when they became aware of people such as Queen making videos, they got into the business and they made some. Like "Closer to the Heart", they were incredibly primitive: just performance stuff in the early years. Later on, of course, they played with all the edges of video: they did a computer-based video, one of the first high-definition videos — one of a series. They're willing to take a chance with anything that could be unique in terms of video.

Interestingly, Rush don't see themselves — and they don't need to — to be an image band. Yet people say that video emphasizes image, that artists will change their music to do their video. Rush proves that's not necessarily true.

Rough Trade, "High School Confidential": Again, here's a case where an artist recognized video's potential and momentum and wanted to be there to play the edges. Carole Pope and Rough Trade have done several videos, including "High School Confidential" that were as risqué as you could possibly get.

What they proved is that you could collapse the selling of an image. Instead of taking three hundred days on the road to meet enough people to show you what we can do, like Rush, you can do that in three minutes. It will work for you.

Triumph, "Blinding Light Show": In 1987, Triumph were invited to be a part of the US Festival in California — one of the largest festivals known to mankind. Rather than just do it and walk away, they thought the thing through — and invited our MuchMusic crew to join them down there. We flew in, backstage on their helicopter, and we taped the whole thing. A band doesn't often get a chance to demonstrate that they played for half-a-million people. Triumph understood that up front.

Part of a metal concert is the spectacle, being there for the event. In fact, the event is almost as important as the band, in some ways. Triumph were very smart about that. They said, "This is who we're going to be: we're going to be big and we're going to bring our light show down." So it made sense for them to demonstrate that they are a band to be taken seriously enough to play to half-a-million people. Instead of ignoring it, they played it.

Eventually, they rolled that into other material and used it as a video for "Blinding Light Show". What the video did for them was to show people how big they were in the US. And it's easy, in Canada, to ignore how big Triumph were in the US. When they did an American metal festival, Triumph, if they weren't the headliner, were always number two behind Motley Crue or whatever. To demonstrate that to Canadians — where there isn't an outlet for that — is difficult. So they used the media and they used video and it was very smart.

Neil Young, "This Note's For You": In a world where people are trying to market rock 'n' roll in the same way that they market sports — and trying to use the leverage that rock 'n' roll has with youth to attract a certain audience and to impress a certain audience, Neil was in a position to be able to sit back and say, "I've never done it, I won't do it. In fact, I

Larry Gowan: a consumate performer

have the balls to actually stand up and shout it." He won't accept sponsors and he doesn't play music because the sponsor asked him to. And this is a gorgeous example of balls, integrity, whatever — that should never have worked if you're cynical enough to believe that money controls rock 'n' roll. It's a very beautiful piece of video.

Glass Tiger, "Don't Forget Me (When I'm Gone)": There were, in fact, two videos done for this song — one for the US market and one for Canada. The reasons for that are fairly simple — and fairly important. In Canada, an inexpensive video can be used to get MuchMusic play, to get Video Hits play. But try to cross over into the American market with that video, and it won't work. The Americans demand another level of sophistication — and at the end of the day, if a video doesn't sell records, there's no point in making it.

The difference between the two is straight production values. The average Canadian video costs, maybe, $40,000. The average American one costs $80,000 American. We live in a world where an advertiser will spend $800,000 on a 30-second spot to provide a certain level of sophistication. That is what a viewer is used to seeing. So when you are making a music video, you can do one of two things: you can sell the band as a rock 'n' roll band, or you can aim for that sophistication. And we've seen videos made for $150 and we've seen videos made for a million and a half dollars. Michael Jackson has spent at least a million and a half dollars several times. On the other hand, my favourite cheap video is made by The Gas in England, who took an extension cord and a Video-8 and stood outside one of the guys' mother's apartment (because that's how far the extension cord went) and shot the video. And made the Guinness Book of Records for the fastest distributed music video in the world because they then duplicated it and had it on the market in about an hour and a half. And that's how they got the media out of it.

But when it comes to the demographic, hard-nosed LA sell, they want the lead singer front and centre so that people can identify with him. I think that's a very short-term kind of way of using video, but that's one of those things that they insist on doing in the States. There, they believe that they must get their money back in terms of record sales. What I have been told is that, for a superstar act, a good video, with good distribution, well-placed, can make the difference between, say, 4 and 5 million albums sold. In other words, you get newsstand value. If an artist has a good video that works at a certain level where it achieves that *People* magazine level, you can go an extra mile — and when you start going those extra miles, with that many zeros, it becomes real money.

Bruce Cockburn, "Rocket Launcher": An inexpensive video that broke new ground because it was the first video that used prerecorded images. News footage, for example, images that were already available and out there. So instead of a straight performance piece, they used war footage from around the world. They used film of Mulroney, Nixon, products. What you got was a social statement in the same way that Bruce meant it — all couched in the kind of images that, as a television viewer, you are used to. I find it important because, beyond that, several people have tried to do the same thing: Michael Jackson did it for "Man in the Mirror". That didn't work; the difference, I guess, is integrity.

Another of Bruce's videos, on the other hand, "Lovers in a Dangerous Time", didn't work for me — or for Bruce — because it was an attempt to make a low-budget, traditional video, if you will, that featured the artist and

BLAST

KLAATU

BACKGROUND:
Toronto-based band consisted of Terry Draper on drums, John Woloschuk on keyboards, and Dee Long on guitar. They all wrote and sang on the five albums they recorded throughout the '70s and early '80s. The band was named for a character in the movie The Day the Earth Stood Still.

CLAIMS TO FAME:
Named "Hype of the Year" by Rolling Stone *in 1977, Klaatu jumped onto the front pages because of the rumour that claimed the band was really The Beatles who had secretly reformed under a different name. The band denied the rumours, but maintained secrecy about their identites. This only further fueled the rumours. Their second album,* Hope, *won a Juno award for best engineered album. Among their biggest singles were "Sub Rosa Subway", the song that got the Beatles rumour rolling, "Dear Christine", and "Knee Deep in Love". The Carpenters' cover version of the Klaatu song "Calling Occupants" went Top 20 in the US and Top 10 in Canada, Japan, and England.*

MUSICAL STYLE:
Progressive pop rock

WHERE ARE THEY NOW?:
Klaatu reunited briefly in 1988 to record a single for a West German television show called Tatort. *The song was recorded in England where Long has a MIDI (musical instrument digital interface) studio. The band is considering an album, and were planning to release their first two albums in CD form. Draper has a roofing business in Oak Ridges, north of Toronto. He also has a studio in his house where he writes, produces, and records songs. He is currently writing a feature film score. Woloschuk is an accountant in Toronto with a number of musicians as clients.*

QUOTABLE QUOTE:
Draper on the Beatles rumour: "The public will believe what it wants to believe. Everyone wanted the Beatles to get back together again, and so they bought the rumour. We were thrilled. This was wonderful because we were all devout Beatle fans, and the ultimate accomplishment was that [being mistaken for them]. We had a good laugh and watched the record sales climb."

FABULOUS FACT:
The Beatles rumour wasn't coincidence; Klaatu intentionally did try to sound like the Beatles on some songs on the first album. Once the truth was out, each album sold less than its predecessor.

dancers and wasn't what I think Bruce Cockburn is about. Bruce Cockburn is about being a poet with a social conscience.

Gowan, "Strange Animal": Gowan is one of those artists who could be faceless. They do great songs, but if you fell over them in the street, you wouldn't know who they were. Gowan, for a lot of people, makes great records, gets great radio play at that point in his career, but he's not necessarily someone that they've seen. Yet Gowan is a great live performer. And like a great live performer, he is a lot more than you would imagine from his records. So the exercise in making "Strange Animal" was to do something that demonstrated who he was as a performer and also to do something in terms of video, and the director, Rob Quartley, found a nice synthesis with computer animation and Gowan doing what he does. The animation is important; it broke new ground.

Pursuit of Happiness, "I'm an Adult Now": Although they subsequently did an updated version of this, the original one was shot, by them, on Queen Street West in Toronto, doing what they do. They were comfortable with their surroundings – comfortable with everything. It was very simply, very nicely put together – and for very little money. They stood up on their own as a band and it worked. Instead, then, of going in a completely different direction in the second version, they tried to recreate it with better production values. And as soon as you start *thinking* about that kind of natural exuberance, it dissipates. The first one was "anything to get it on to the television" and to get the name out there. It was done quite naturally and as cheaply as they could do it and then banged off and there it was. The second one feels much more mannered. Making a great video is like being a great actor. Anyone can act once. You then try and recreate that character, and if you're not a good actor, you'll never find it again. If you are a great actor, that's called craft.

**Payola$**, "China Girl": There was a show in Vancouver, on cable, that was doing music videos and making music videos. And helping people in the community make music videos. So one day I'm sitting at my desk in Toronto feeling kind of alone in the world – and a guy called Ed Mulberry walks into the office and dumps on my desk a number of music videos with intros and extros and hellos and the whole bit from Vancouver. The stuff included pieces by D.O.A., endorsements by Joey Shithead and a couple of great videos – including "China Girl" by the Payola$, an inexpensively made video by a group of people who considered themselves as internationally smart as any of the punk or the new wave people in England. It was marvelous material.

You know, there are two levels of rock and roll. One of them is the corporate level and then there are the mates that talk amongst themselves. And these guys in Vancouver were incredibly on top of what was happening in Europe – have discovered what it could do for people in Europe and were using it in Vancouver. And then distributed it themselves.

The Box, "Closer Together": It's very difficult for an English artist to break out in Montreal. I guess they don't have the naturally inherent support of the music community there. Yet The Box managed to make it in Montreal. They made the decision to record in English – to go international – and how do you do that? You can do that piece by piece on radio or you can make a video. And they've made several and they're all really good – because he is an artist. Whatever media he's using, he has some kind of inherent strength. So his videos have

BLAST

JACK LONDON

BACKGROUND:
Jack London and his band The Sparrow got their start in Oshawa, Ont., and, thanks to vocalist London being from England, were able to cash in on the British Invasion of the early '60s. London, whose real name is Dave Marden, was joined by a number of musicians who played in the band including Nick St. Nicholas, Jerry and Dennis Edmonton (a.k.a. Mars Bonfire), who all went on to play in Steppenwolf.

CLAIMS TO FAME:
The band hit number 1 on many radio stations with "If You Don't Want My Love", and also scored with "I'll Be The Boy" and "Meet Me After Four". They were one of the most popular groups in Yorkville in the mid-'60s.

MUSICAL STYLE:
British-sounding rock. Minus London, the Sparrow later played bluesy rock.

WHERE IS HE NOW:
Marden did some producing after leaving The Sparrow, dabbled in business, and is now president of the Canadian Association of Real Estate Investors, as well as of his own company, Dave Marden Real Estate Inc., located in Whitby, Ont. He is planning to publish a book on real estate investment in 1989, and estimates his real estate holdings at more than $1 million. Marden also sings occasionally in Oshawa, where he lives, and plans to open a small recording studio in 1989, the 25th anniversary of his professional start in singing. He is writing songs and has plans for a musical about the Yorkville music scene of the '60s.

QUOTABLE QUOTE:
Marden on his very occasional singing gigs: "I'll get up and sing a few tunes and these grey-haired ladies will come up and say I knew you as Jack London when you were first starting. The fact is I would rather have done it and left it, than to have never done it."

FABULOUS FACT:
Marden took the name Jack London from the famous novelist, and also because it suggested a British band. The Sparrow name was chosen partly as a response to Ronnie Hawkins' band The Hawks. Ironically, both bands became more famous under other names, Steppenwolf and The Band respectively.

always been smart in a world where sometimes you get commercial directors making videos that have nothing to do with the artist.

Joni Mitchell, "My Secret Place": A very nice video. She had managed to work with Peter Gabriel on the album, *Chalkmark in a Rainstorm* and that made the single sound nice, but did it necessarily identify her in a punter's mind with Peter Gabriel, who is enjoying a certain amount of success? But if you put them together in a video and you can see them together, enjoying each other, enjoying the fact that they are working together and that they share a certain lyrical dream — I think it does terrific things for her. And what's obvious in the video is that they share a dream — they share an artistic vision. Neither of them look uncomfortable in the video. So that slops over that they felt like that in the studio — and that was what the track was about. And if you're a Peter Gabriel fan who's not necessarily a Joni Mitchell fan, you might make the leap.

Barney Bentall, "Heart's on Fire": Barney Bentall is a good example of the effect of geography on rock 'n' roll in Canada. He's a local artist with enormous respect in Vancouver. So he made a video very cheaply — an independent video of this great song. He got it played on MuchMusic and, interestingly enough, it was picked up by a record company. They turned around and made a video with better production values — and it is a better video. This is all in Canada. It isn't like suddenly we flipped into megadollars in the United States. This is a very cheap performance video by Barney with a great song. Barney is the most appealing guy on the planet. So it was simple enough that you learned that from the video. It's a good example of what can happen by using video as a demo tape.

Of course, there is a downside to all this: if the A&R guys are watching TV that means they probably aren't getting out to the clubs anymore — which is a pain in the butt.

John Martin is program director for MuchMusic, The Nation's Music Station.

13 ESSENTIAL DISCS

by Alan Guettel

Honeymoon Suite: teenage angst

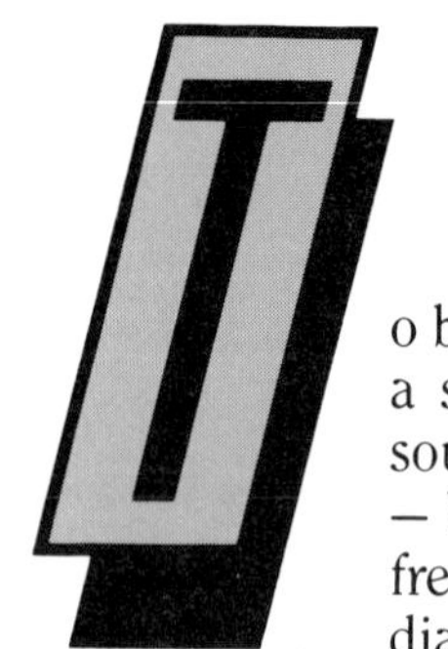

To be a hit, the irony goes, a song or an act has to sound like all the others — but it also must sound fresh and original. Canadian acts meet the first requirement by being able to sound more or less like anything that comes from the United States or Great Britain. Call this "The Rich Little Syndrome" of Canadian pop culture. But when Canadian music succeeds, pop musicians have generally fulfilled the second requirement by embracing — or not being able to avoid — national features and historical accidents that come with being from Canada. This discography offers an account of the many ways Canadian recording artists have found niches in the big picture by each bringing something special from Canada to the marketplace of real pop music.

The guy groups were first: The Four Lads, The Crew Cuts, and The Diamonds. These were congenial Toronto boys, most good Catholics, who sang mostly laundered Black with choir-boy sweetness for US audiences. In practical terms, they were part of the American business. Their careers in no way resembled those of later Canadian pop acts — who would write their own songs, play their own instruments, often run their own careers, and, most importantly, slowly build a pop-music business here in Canada. In the '80s, Attic Records picked up the rights to 12 classic guy-group singles tracks — including "Sh-Boom", "Little Darlin'", and "Moments To Remember". (Attic Records, LAT-1209).

Anka's 21 Greatest Hits (RCA Victor LPM 2691): As much as we now think Paul Anka's early songs sound juvenile, he gets a lot of credit for being one of the first singers of the era to write his own songs and thus control his career. That's how he survived all the American Bobbies and Jimmies of his day.

Ian and Sylvia: *Great Speckled Bird* (Ampex A101103), Ian and Sylvia's *Four Strong*

Sweeney Todd: operatic ambitions

Winds album would be on my list of 30 monumental American albums of the past 30 years, but their Canadian seminal album is *Great Speckled Bird* because that showed that they were re-investing their careers here. Thank God.

Ronnie Hawkins, *The Hawk* (Hawk Records GRT9205-9039); and *The Best of Ronnie Hawkins* (Roulette 9045-42045): Ronnie Hawkins came up from Arkansas and rocked up the sleepy Canadian scene in the early '60s. But his real Canadianization came in the '70s. He still paid the rent doing the old R&B licks (maybe a little more Rich Little than Little Richard here) and being Bob Dylan's friend, and the only guy to be on the soundtrack of *American Graffitti* and *The Last Waltz*.

Gordon Lightfoot, *Lightfoot* (United Artists UAS6487): The most significant feature of Lightfoot's huge recorded corpus is that he's never surprised, he's never gone outside of what he does better than everybody else.

Joni Mitchell, *Clouds* (Reprise RS 6341): Joni Mitchell's seminal albums are mostly products of her rich American experience. But *Clouds* was embraced here as Canadian – the product of a Prairie girl who had no place to work out her ideas except inside her own head.

Neil Young, *Rust Never Sleeps* (Reprise XHS 2295): Nobody *likes* Neil Young. His fans love him; others can't see what the fuss is all about. But his style – and that whiney voice that Americans seem to find normal – was honed during his days with The Mynah Birds and such in Yorkville. Young's crowning album is *Rust Never Sleeps*; it shows that after Buffalo Springfield of the '60s, Crosby, Stills Nash, and Young of the '70s, the Neil Young of the '80s is going to be a real survivor.

Blood, Sweat and Tears, *Blood Sweat and Tears* (Columbia CS 9720): David Clayton Thomas developed his act by deftly immitating American R&B singers. He then spectacularly led an American band to greatness. The first *Blood Sweat and Tears* album was one of the most impressive and original pop albums any Canadian has ever been associated with in any way.

Mandala, *Classics* (WEA 25 23921): Mandala (main members: Domenic Troiano and George Olliver) left a significant legacy of singles that were released in the mid-'80s as *Classics*. "Opportunity" (recorded at Chess Studios in Chicago with The Dells singing backup) rose to #3 on the CHUM chart, behind "Ruby Tuesday" and "Green, Green Grass Of Home". And that was before the Canadian airplay rules.

Anne Murray, *Honey Wheat and Laughter* (Capitol ST 6350); *Country* (Capitol ST 6425): Anne Murray was the first brand new star to rise with the Canadian-content requirements. Her producer, Brian Ahern, mixed proven hit songs with songs from unknown Canadian songwriters on her LPs. That was good for business, and it made good listening. Her second album, *Honey Wheat and Laughter*, and the later repackage of her early country-flavoured hits also combined good business and good listening.

Bruce Cockburn, *Waiting for a Miracle* (True North TN2K-67): Although Bruce Cockburn's early records are dear and intelligent – and classics in this country – it's the later albums that show a Canadian road to commercial success: sincerity and patience. When anger, rebellion, conscience, and revolution had become as cliched as "I love you" in most pop music, a mature Cockburn emerged who stood out because he really meant it. *Stealing Fire* (True North

BLAST

MASHMAKHAN

BACKGROUND:
The members of Mashmakhan were Rayburn Blake, guitar, Pierre Senecal, keyboards, Brian Edwards, vocals, and Jerry Mercer, drums. These Montreal musicians played in a variety of bands throughout the '60s, notably Triangle before their big success in 1970.

CLAIMS TO FAME:
Known primarily for their #1 song, "As The Years Go By", the group released other singles, such as "Children of the Sun", which didn't match the success of the first. "As The Years Go By" was one of the biggest selling singles ever in Japan. The band was named after a plant that grows in Bermuda called "match-me-if-you-can".

MUSICAL STYLE:
Pop-rock

WHERE ARE THEY NOW?:
Blake heads the multi-track recording department of Steve's Music Store in Toronto, and also plays in a duo with Frankie Hart called Touche, doing Top 40ish material, Senecal performed for several years in Moncton, N.B., moved to Montreal in 1987, and does production work. Mercer played drums for April Wine after leaving Mashmakhan, performed with Montreal group The Buzz Band, and with April Wine alumnus Brian Greenway. His latest band is called Big City, a band that plays early '70s style rock. Edwards was last heard to be living and performing in Saskatchewan.

QUOTABLE QUOTES:
Blake on their #1 hit: "It was a one-of-a-kind song. People who remember it were much younger than I was at the time, people eight or nine years old. And that's a good feeling. I'm not going to knock that." Senecal: "I remember when I wrote that song I felt I had something that was extremely commercial."

FABULOUS FACT:
Senecal, who still speaks with a thick French-Canadian accent, has never written a French song because he finds English phrasing much easier. "As The Years Go By" apparently took him 15 minutes to write.

TN 57) broke through internationally on the industry's own terms, with videos and all. But for a complete Cockburn retrospective, the compact disc with 33 Cockburn songs from 1970-1987, *Waiting For A Miracle,* says it all.

Murray McLauchlan, *Sweeping The Spotlight Away* (True North TN-18): McLauchlan is a unique songwriter because he is a chronicler of outward images and other people rather than of tedious personal feelings. *Sweeping The Spotlight Away* proved he was a national asset. His *Greatest Hits* LP in 1978 (True North TN35) is still the greatest greatest-hits album of the era.

The Guess Who, *Wheatfield Soul* (RCA ANL 1171): This album most signified the coming of age of the pop business. Small-city guys who learned the craft imitating American pop singers on a CBC teens TV show proved they eventually could do it better themselves.

The Band, *Northern Lights, Southern Cross* (Capitol ST-11440): You can't leave out The Band. Though *Music From Big Pink* has to be on any American significant LPs list, and *The Last Waltz* presents more Canadian greats than any but a K-Tel record, their primo Canadian album is *Northern Lights Southern Cross* because it took that long (1975) for the mainstream biz here to catch up with them. And the cut "Acadian Driftwood" – Robbie Robertson's rewrite of "The Night They Drove Old Dixie Down", about the losers of our war of conquest – went to the heart of our mythology.

Downchild Blues Band, *Downchild So Far* (Posterity PTR 13004): Downchild kept it together by never playing less than solid blues in the best and worst Canadian bars. And they didn't need an American to front them. *Downchild So Far,* a best-of album of 1977, is one of those albums that you can listen to right through and still smell the stale beer.

Rough Trade, *Rough Trade Live* (Umbrella UMB DD1) proved that there was a cult road to success in Canada, if the cult grows big enough. Carole Pope and Kevin Staples put together an outrageous send-up of the streetwise and the carnal arts that often fooled their bizarre audiences – and sometimes themselves. Their *Rough Trade Live* looks and sounds like a special-edition piece of art.

Bachman-Turner Overdrive, *Japan Tour Live* (Mercury SRM 1 3703): was the last of the Canadian bands made up of guys old enough to have learned their chops before The Beatles. *Japan Tour Live* shows the gut power that band had.

The Quebec Bands that hit big brought something unique to rock – and rock brought something unique to them. Before the '70s, Quebec pop stars either sang in a tradition removed from the mainstream or sang silly translations of American hits. But the new wave of rockers boomed in the '70s by mangling their own language and styled into the basic 4/4 iambic pentameter of rock 'n' roll. That created an edge that made their rock sound appropriately dangerous, just when so much 'white' rock was going mainstream. Representative breakthrough albums are: *Robert Charlebois* (Gamma GM/GS 115), *Beau Dommage* (Capitol ST 70034), and Harmonium's *L'heptade* (CBS PGF 90348).

Michel Pagliaro, *Aujourd'hui* (Columbia PFS 90384): Michel Pagliaro's career reads like a storybook: In the early '70s, he was a popsie who mixed French covers of English songs with some cute ones of his own. He even went English for a while. But his 1977 *Aujourd'hui* is French – and real rock 'n' roll in any language.

Kate and Anna McGarrigle, *Kate and Anna McGarrigle* (Warner Bros. BS 2862): More folkie, Kate and Anna McGarrigle sing in both French and English, and fans from coast to coast will never stop playing their first album that includes "Heart Like A Wheel."

By the late '70s, there was little more pioneering left to do in the recording industry. Bands were expected to have big hits, and the business was in place to make that happen.

By the mid-'70s, bands broke big; it seemed that the first time you ever heard them, they were on top of the charts, e.g., Rush, *All The World's A Stage* (Mercury SRM 2 7508), April Wine, *April Wine* (Aquarius AQR502), Triumph, *Triumph* (Attic IAT 1012), and Sweeney Todd, *Sweeney* (London PS 664). They were expected to fill huge arenas and sell lots of records to long-haired American white working-class boys. And they did.

By the '80s, the successors to these bands were even created by investors, and their formula rock' piled up some of our biggest sales figures ever, e.g., Streetheart, *Live After Dark* (Capitol ST2 6507) and Loverboy, *Get Lucky* (Columbia FC 37638).

And in the late '80s yet another generation of kids, born since the Beatles broke up, are gobbling up records by the new wave of pretty-boy suburban bands. They look good in videos. They come from Anywhere, USA – which in their case happens to be Canada, e.g., Glass Tiger, *Thin Red Line,* (Capitol ST 6527), Honeymoon Suite, *The Big Prize* (WEA 2528241), and Platinum Blonde, *Standing In The Dark,* (CBS PCC 80090).

But there still are actual stars being ground out from the Canadian experience. Bryan Adams, *You Want It – You Got It,* (A&M SP 4864) would have been a star in any era. His songs work even inside the narrow restrictions of today's pop. And k.d. lang. She's put together cult, class, and promo to latch onto a fast career – but her very modest first album is one of those rare records where you drop the needle anywhere and say, "This girl can sing!"

To conclude, two new oldies. Leonard Cohen never intended to be a musician, and he isn't. He found a special niche by using poetic angst to somehow bridge the gap between prematurely aged post-adolescents and mid-life males. His new album, *I'm Your Man* (CBS FC/CK 44191) brought a lot of over-40s to the record store for the first time in a decade. The same with Robbie Robertson *Gatten,* (CD/XGHS 24160). Maybe there'll be more than nostalgia for the currently middle-aged.

Alan Guettel is a record archivist and producer at the CBC.

BLAST

THE BEAU-MARKS

BACKGROUND:
The Beau-Marks hailed from Montreal, and original members included Joe Frechette, piano, Ray Hutchinson, guitar, Mike Robitaille, bass, and Gilles Tailleur, drums. The band took their name from the controversial Bomarc missile of the 1950s. Frechette lives in Oshawa, Hutchinson and Robitaille are still in Montreal. Tailleur died of a cerebral hemorrhage when he was 35.

CLAIMS TO FAME:
Their biggest hit was "Clap Your Hands", which, in 1960, reached Number 1 in Canada, Australia, and New Zealand. It fell just short of the Top 40 in the US. Other notable singles were "Billy, Billy Went A-Walking", "Classmate", "Little Miss Twist", and "The Tender Years". The group also appeared on Dick Clark's American Bandstand show.

MUSICAL STYLE:
Rock-and-roll and ballads

WHERE ARE THEY NOW?
Frechette is program director at country radio station CHOO in Ajax, Ont., and released a remake of "Clap Your Hands" in 1987, which got airplay across Canada and did especially well in the Maritimes. Hutchinson had a successful solo career after leaving The Beau-Marks. In recent years, he sang nightly at Montreal's Le Sentiment restaurant, which he owned. However, in March 1988 he was involved in a serious car accident in Florida and was in a coma for six weeks. He returned to the music business in the fall. Robitaille works as a video producer in Montreal.

QUOTABLE QUOTES:
Frechette on "Clap Your Hands": "The rhythm was right, the tempo was right for dancing. Also people told me that I had a very good tape voice. My voice came off as being very commercial. Ray Hutchinson (the band's lead singer on most songs) sounded great in clubs doing ballads; but when he recorded on tape, he didn't seem to catch on with people's ears."

Hutchinson: "If we only knew how great we were. We didn't know the magic we had, and the potential we had. We were too young. There was magic in that group, and we weren't aware of it."

FABULOUS FACT:
The "Clap Your Hands" record has a "false ending" and then Frechette says "don't go away" before completing the song. Even though Dick Clark was aware of the false ending, he inadvertently walked on camera during the Beau-Marks' performance on his show. He had to jump off camera when they continued singing; viewers thought that it was all pre-planned.

PHOTOGRAPHS SUPPLIED BY:

A & M RECORDS/*Page 145;* BRUCE ALLEN TALENT/*Page 180;* ATTIC RECORDS/*Pages 28, 187;* BMG MUSIC CANADA INC./*Pages 129, 189;* CBC TV/*Pages 41, 83;* CBS PRESS & PUBLICITY/ *Pages 73, 146, 203;* CANADA WIDE FEATURE SERVICES LIMITED/*Pages 11, 14, 16, 21, 27, 30, 31, 32, 34, 35, 37, 39, 45, 47, 48, 49, 51, 53, 57, 61, 65, 70, 77, 89, 95, 99, 105, 109, 115, 117, 119, 143, 149, 151, 155, 157, 171, 173, 175, 177, 183, 185, 193, 195, 196, 199, 205;* CANADIAN TALENT INTERNATIONAL/*Page 66;* CAPITOL RECORDS – EMI OF CANADA/*Pages 29, 67;* DUKE STREET RECORDS/*Pages 69, 103;* HOMESTEAD PRODUCTIONS/*Pages 36, 192;* PHILIP KAMIN/*Pages 5, 79, 101, 178, 179, 188, 189, 191, 209, 217;* OCEAN STUDIOS/*Page 81;* PONO PRESSE/*Pages 43, 50, 54;* CAROLE POPE/*Page 25;* LORRAINE SEGATO/*Pages 38, 123;* SHAW MUSIC/*Page 176;* WEA MUSIC OF CANADA/*Pages 18, 20, 64, 75, 127.*

* * *

"BLAST" PHOTOS, Mark Kearney and Randy Ray

Goddard & Kamin Inc. is one of the world's leading packagers and publishers of mass market books. Peter Goddard and Philip Kamin first got together in 1981 for a book on the Rolling Stones' last tour. Since then they have combined to produce more than 50 titles.